HATED
FOR THE
GODS

HATED FOR THE GODS

poems by

Sean Patrick Mulroy

Button Publishing Inc.
Minneapolis
2023

HATED FOR THE GODS
POETRY
AUTHOR: Sean Patrick Mulroy
COVER DESIGN: Jamie Hudalla
COVER ART CREDIT: Randomagus

◇

◇

Published by Button Poetry
Minneapolis, MN 55418 | http://www.buttonpoetry.com

Manufactured in the United States of America
PRINT ISBN: 978-1-63834-071-3
EBOOK ISBN: 978-1-63834-072-0
AUDIOBOOK ISBN: 978-1-63834-073-7

First printing

versions of these poems first appeared in the following publications: *fair* IMPOSSIBLE ARCHETYPE; *villanelle for the wound* WINNING WRITERS; *it gets better, by halves* THE GOOD MEN PROJECT; *sacrament* ASSARACUS.

my brothers, for you and you alone.

Contents

HATED
FOR THE
GODS

Rightly speaking, to cut a man's flesh after he is dead is far less hateful than to oppress him whilst he lives.

—Robert Louis Stevenson

Tell the people that homosexuals are no cowards.

—Willem Arondeus

fetish

Leather braided into leather, bound
into a cord and dyed night dark—
                    I don't remember
where I bought the bullwhip, only
how it hung
            suspended from a hook
screwed through the ceiling
of my first apartment, clearly visible
as you walked in the front door.

It stayed there like a talisman against
those who might judge my   *lifestyle*,
as it was sometimes called
in those days, though I was a virgin
        and the S&M just decoration—

except once, when twisted up on x
and dextromethorphan I got a friend
                to lick my shoulders
with the whip's black tongue.
It felt good, and I loved the sound
        it made against my naked back.
Like someone gave my skin a voice
            and it was laughing.

sacrament

Here's the thing about a bunch of teenagers
praying in the basement of a church:
  more than grape juice watered-down
    and transubstantiated into wine,
      more than torn flesh of a grocery store baguette
        passed solemnly from faithful hand to faithful hand,
      I take and eat of these, their lives
    which shall be given up for Him
and bury them within me.
Even as a grown man, lying here
beside my lover, naked
in the bed of our hotel room,
soaking stale toast in a cheap merlot—
  I know they're here.
  They're watching.

Erin with the port-wine stain, who asks me, teary-eyed,
Do you think we will recognize each other when we get to heaven?

  Bad-teeth bully Curtis with the untrimmed beard
  who gathers me to his beginnings of a beer gut saying,
  Oh, I've done you so much wrong.

Tonight, I hold my lover's bird-thin body
underneath the sheets and I remember Nathan,
  whom I loved. How frail he seemed
    inside his blue Jawbreaker t-shirt.
    How surprised I was to be
    allowed to run my palms against
    the bones of his most sacred back
as we embraced each other
in Christ's love after Communion.
How I imagined for a second
  God might be there
    creating all the miracles of touch
    before he pulled away.

note pinned to the natural science cabin
Camp Goshen, 1997

Dear Todd and Jake,

    You are the best counselors I've ever had ever. I wanted to say you are way nicer than the Indian Lore counselors who are always telling me not to eat the corn or the pemmican and are always reading dirty stories about Coyote taking out his penis except they won't talk about it in front of me because they said I'm just a little kid. I only know because I heard it later from a guy in Troop 1916. I know I was mad when you fed the snake a mouse and made me watch, but it's ok. I know the snake has to eat too. I'm sad I didn't get to say goodbye, but that's not important right now. All that matters is telling the people you ~~love~~ like how you feel. You guys are the best! I'll always remember you!

    You, Todd, with your face a savage field of acne scars, and you, Jake, picking up the white mouse by its tail, your tongue's rough slide across your scaly lips. The both of you, just watching terror scratching at the glass of the terrarium, a feral wailing wrapped then crushed with glutted muscles, swallowed still alive by coils blacker than the pupil of an open eye—

My First Date

Matt and I kiss for the first time
    in the Back Bay Fens, beneath a tree.

It's night, and I've just asked
if he knows what a shotgun is.

He says no,
                so I take a long drag
on the pipe packed full of dank weed
and I let the smoke curl past my lips
           like ivy down his throat.
That's a shotgun, I say,
         pressing my forehead against his.
He smiles.
         Steam escapes him in a sigh.

His teeth catch moonlight, then the azure wailing
of a siren as a cop car roars off Boylston and skids
         across the grass into the park.

We split apart.

Matt chucks the bowl.

We try to walk away as casually as possible, but
then the floodlight snaps on and the officer says
through his radio,
         FREEZE

This is my first date.

§

People like to say

    The Gay Rights Movement started with a riot.

It did not.

           There were plenty of us working
peacefully toward the right to love each other openly—
that is, authentically exist whilst un-imprisoned and,
with any luck, employed—
years before the word   *homosexual*   was invented.

We like to remember Stonewall because
that's the first time we took on the cops
                       and won.

A momentary triumph, sandwiched between
   years and years spent on our knees before
   the throbbing billy clubs of boys in blue.

Even in the bars and neighborhoods we claimed as ours,
                we were too unruly to be left ignored,
that is, unbeaten, until the plague came
and the bruises surfaced from the inside.

Then, it seems, we were a problem
                better left unmanaged.

But alas, you've come for poetry,
            and found instead a screed.

        I'll start over.

§

Underneath a tree, I kiss a boy
whose leather jacket is still warm
from inside the apartment where we scored
the weed that haunts the space between
              our mouths.

The year is 2001.

Matt and I met on a dating website,
one designed specifically for gay minors
in search of love.
                    I'm 17 and scared
to meet a stranger,
                    so I've brought a chaperone.
Her name is Laura, but she goes by Desdemona.

            She's the one who sold us weed.

When the police cruiser lurches through the darkness
toward our bodies, Desdemona is the one
                    who does the talking.

When he asks us if we have drugs,
            she swears we were only smoking cigarettes.

He says,
        Alright, then. In the future, look at it from my perspective, guys.
        I see you in the park, behind a tree. What am I supposed to think?

After the cop leaves, we take a few minutes to find
            Matty's piece, half-buried in the rough.

For the rest of the night we debate whether or not
            the cop knew we were smoking weed.

Because we are (all three of us) white,
            we do so from outside of prison.

§

All systems are inherently fascist—let me explain:

In order for there to be organization, there must be a hierarchy.
Such hierarchies
            are self-servingly constructed by the powerful and few.

(We like to think here in America we have
bypassed this hierarchal problem through
a meritocratic economic system and
electoral democracy, but
with all due respect,   lol.)

The marginalized

(i.e. the not-straight, not-white, not-male, not-cis, not-wealthy)

had no direct hand in the writing or construction of our Republic.
Since then, a lucky few have not so much been given power
               as we have been given access to power.
Like all instances of the word *access*,
                         a price is here implied.

This is not a system my people invented, but it is one in which we
can thrive if we can afford to stay disciplined and inconspicuous,

                                    that is, silent and unseen.

§

Matt and I met on a dating website.
Every man I've ever dated entered my life artificially.

    It's more common now for straight couples to meet
through apps or online personals, but for the homosexual
this has been the norm for decades.

    The alternatives were dangerous.

    Public cruising spots, mostly, and these,
    riddled with muggers, thieves, and last,
    but certainly not least,
                         police.

The internet arrived and drained the backrooms and park benches
                    of their pesky public sex.
It organized the cruise park into an electronic system,

13

replaced knowing glances, sweaty palms,
and raw necessity, with racy photographs of pornographic bodies.
These bodies are most often able, cis, and white.

They skew toward men with memberships
to fancy gyms, access to trainers, healthy food—

Access.

Money.

Power.

Hierarchy.

Most young gay men were born to a world
of public emptinesses they don't know enough about
                                          to mourn.
        How could they know?

The generation before mine and Matt's
was more than decimated by disease.
                              It was obliterated.
Before we were old enough to claim
a culture meant to be our birthright,
            it was bought out from beneath the piles of our dead.

We grew up in a vacuum first,   and then a grid.

Who would tell us of our wild history?
Our long-standing association with the Civil Rights Movement?
Our roots in anti-capitalist activism?

Billionaire straight men owned *The Advocate.*

They owned *Out Magazine.*

They still own *Grindr.*

§

Oh man, this part of the park is safe, but see that tall grass over there?

Matt points just across the river from our tree.

Don't go there unless you're trying to get molested by a bunch of dirty old men.

He laughs.
I say,   *Eew, gross.*

Desdemona packs the bowl.
We all smoke weed.

Matt and I kiss.

When the cop car roars toward us,
Des is hidden by a low-slung branch.

The three of us then try to scatter
casually, but   *FREEZE*   in the unthinkably bright
spotlight of the cop car. Desdemona does the talking.

Haloed by the law, she's striking, eyes blue as the siren.
Seeing her, the officer's demeanor changes.
He says,
            Alright, then, and drives away.

There's no way he could have missed
the smell of reefer in the air, but that
was never his concern.

Matt and I, alone.

Behind a tree.

A deep kiss.

Tall grass close enough to hear it shuffle in the breeze.

What was he supposed to think?

sex dream in which Tu'er Shen's a no-show

You spend all day getting your house ready for the party,
setting up a table for the potluck with a stack of paper plates
and napkins, pushing your red couch against the wall to make
a little room for dancing.

Right on time, the doorbell rings.
Your guests arrive in groups of two or three, while you
stand waiting by the door. He ought to be here soon.

You never realized until now how much all your friends talk
about love. Every time their conversation turns to sex, or
a romantic movie or a bad date, you imagine him beside you,
nibbling on crudité, his long ears twitching to attention.

The night goes off without a hitch, and everyone has fun.
Most of them stay later than they'd planned.
Eventually, the last few grab their coats.
You lead them out. Thank them for coming.
                    Then the house is quiet.

You lie down on a lawn chair in the backyard by the pool
and spark a joint. You check your phone
        and see he's sent a text, just one word: *Sorry*
    Inside you are empty places filling up
    with smoke, and maybe you don't love him after all—
    or maybe there is nothing you love more than how
    a man can make you suffer just by staying away.

The summer touches you in all the places you hoped
he might, and you swell with your own heat remembering
his long eyelashes brushed against you at the ilium.
    Above your head, a line of paper lanterns glows
            the red-orange of ripe peaches, throbbing
            like a blurry strand of beating hearts.
    When you are hurt, you feel yours swell and ebb
                    within you, keeping you alive.
That's how you know it's real, though you have never seen it.
                    Never held it in your hand.

the evidence speaks for itself

Cave Painting, 11,000 BCE

I swim the labyrinthine aeons, through
the languid black of suffocated blood
in veins of ore and weathering, I wait
like crime-scene fingerprint to be revealed,
to meet the daylight in Addaura, where
a man left silhouettes of what he loved.
Long after he has sifted into dirt
and nothingness will I, an image sketched
in hematite and manganese, survive.
Two lovers arch their naked backs amidst
a ring of dancing eagle-headed gods,
their bodies wrangling, cocks hard. I endure
millennia of storm and flood and quake
to be assailed by scholars, suddenly
fastidious for proof he could not leave.

It's different

Yes, I once believed it too, with all my heart: that love would be the death of me. I still believe with half. We've been first dead for millennia in war and on the television, with no safe place, not really. Not in our homes, or at our jobs, or in our own damn nightclubs; not at art shows, or at open mics, or in our mother's kitchen. While all studies of the human psyche would suggest shame to be more harmful than fists, there are fists, still. Fuck you. Fists, still. Typecast as a villain until everyone agreed. Domestic terror in our blood cells, history policed—they call it *bromance* if they don't read books, *Romantic Friendship* if they do. Addiction, suicide, a dozen times a dozen bottles drowned. A scream inside an abalone, ghost wealth buttressing your prejudice, but some people are poor, and fags are people, even if our personhood is *different*. As you are so often fond of saying when
it doesn't make you wrong,   *America is not the world.*
              I've seen the world.
I've kissed in secret rooms, and danced in secret rooms, and sweat in secret rooms, and fucked in secret rooms, and lived the wet and messy life of men sequestered in our secret rooms, clandestine by necessity, the door chained and then locked from the outside and every day some hand to swing a key like hypnotist while naming us such sneaky little thieves.
You're right. It *is* different—just not in the way you mean, which is essentially a coward's version of
                              It's not as bad,

    or *It's not bad enough for me to come correct,*

    or *I don't care for liberation unless it directly benefits me,*

    or *I only care for liberation when it does numbers on social,*

    or *I only pretend to care about liberation when not caring gets me cancelled,*

    or *Fuck you, faggot. I'll say what I want.*

                              What are you going to do about it?

jolly boys

Rob and I became friends when I stole a bunch of Percocet from someone and was so lonely I gave it all away for free. He used to come by my place and we'd lie down on the carpet, staring up at the acoustic tiles on the ceiling, each the same dull shade of eggshell as the pills we crushed up and inhaled until our faces bloomed to cold bouquets of frost white lilies. We stayed friends because we never slept together and because we loved and hated all the same things: ourselves, our parents, our bodies, our school, our city, employment. We were every open bar's worst nightmare— too polite to get thrown out and too speedy to pass out. We kicked down the door to Allston house parties like crazy, tattooed versions of the guys on Dragnet, confiscating all the booze and all the drugs and pistol-whipping some head senseless on our way out. There were nights we paced the streets like coked-up lions, chain-smoking and talking about art, and if I told you that Rob was to me the loudest music in those days of dirty basement shows and ditch weed, I would not be lying.

When he left town, I stopped going out. I played my guitar alone in my apartment until it was time to go to work at Blockbuster. I dropped 30lbs and started writing poetry. Eventually I left too, if only to get away from life without him there. It has been 20 years and we don't see much of each other and I worry it's because he thinks I was in love with him. I wasn't.

What I loved: Playing songs so high I couldn't plug my Strat into the amp. Rob tipping the bottle to my lips. The night we threw my roommate's dishes off the roof. Speeding down I-90, steadying the steering wheel for him while he took shots of vodka. Huffing paint markers until I passed out on his stairs. The man he made of me. The bachelor party on the night before his wedding, just the two of us and two cigars, a dock in Yonkers. Rob, my only brother. A tobacco burn across my lips. A pitcher full of coffee, bottle full of pills, the music pouring from us hot and sweet as liquor set on fire. How it mattered.

How he made me believe all of it, each second, mattered.

nowhere

That boy is way too pretty to look so sad.

—Chris Alvarez to my friend Kixie, in reference to me
while I waited in line to rent bowling shoes

16 and so many ways to be in danger—
        white trash boys, their lead pipe bodies raised
against my hunger, parents overacting their confusion
at the makeup on my face, the lowing of the diesel engine
in my dinged-up Benz, a relic
swerving into traffic in a blur of chrome and midnight,
speakers coughing Hole and Sonic Youth.
    I want to be one of Araki's boys, the shoegaze drone
    slow flowing through their installation art bedrooms,
    their t-shirts ripped up and revealing skin soaked wet
    in technicolor light, their speech
                        a dialect of 90s queer and LA cool.
My girl wants me to meet Chris, shortstack Latinx faggot,
a high school drop-out with a hot pink fauxhawk.
It is 4PM when we show up, and he's still crawling
out of bed with smudged eyeliner,
thick ass stuffed in tight black jeans.
I wait, and watch him sift through piles of laundry
            on his floor to find the perfect shirt to wear
            on our date at the local bowling alley.
Sweet kid,   flat broke in suburbia and begging me
                        to let him buy my cheese fries.
Teenage queen,
so soon to be abandoned at the driveway's
                    mouth unkissed, and never called again.
    Oh, Chris.   Delightful mischief in your dark eyes
                    glittering, but I am drowned, too deep
in the water to be rescued with a line—
and I'm not even sad the whole way yet.

                                I'm just getting started.

zippo

The summer before you got sick,
    the local farms were gassing all their barns
for bats, illegally. Their bodies small and weak
and littering the ground
            with wrinkled leather wings
            pinned underneath their arms
            like ruined kites.
They hated to be seen,
    exaggerated fury gnarling their faces
    at the flick of my brass zippo, our eyes
as we peered down at them to watch
as they crawled on the brick steps
        to your dorm.

We wondered where they'd come from.

        If they'd really all die.

Later we blew lines of dope off text books
    from your last semester, made out
in the kitchen of a kegger somewhere
off-campus to light sorority applause.

My shirt sweat through and skin a lunar shade
of white, I threw up in the bushes three times
    on the way back to your room where you
    helped me get undressed and into bed,
    your palm pressed to my forehead,
    tender as a nurse.

Winter,
    when you called and told me to get tested.

I was in the back room
of the failing video store
where I worked,
        mop in hand, my uniform
      two sizes too small, no name tag.

My boss had no idea that I was gay, or why
I had to leave before my shift was over.

It was Friday night; in those days,
        all the Boston clinics
                shuttered for the weekend—
so I drank tequila in the shower,
thinking of the bats,
their writhing death
in the July heat from a lawless poison,
corpses spilled
across the grass
                like withered leaves.
That morning, we loved so hard
we broke your headboard.
I made you keep your combat boots on
so I wouldn't miss my train.

                        We cut it close.
I barely caught it at the station,
whistle blowing
                as I ran across the track.

the evidence speaks for itself
Cave Painting, 8000 BCE

Beneath the ground as ghostly seed we too
await the flurried rain of shoveled earth.
Exhumed, we are as shadowed vines that bloom
as quickly as we are denied, we three
who walked the dry sand and savanna grass
now bordering the cliff's edge of mankind's
capricious memory. We ancestors
to Africans and therefore all the world,
whose Rorschached likenesses are wed by rope-
         length phallus draped across a mural like
a strand of molten sugar, are too sweet
to be acknowledged predecessors of
those kneeling to a colonizer's god,
     who bend to kiss the white jackboot of Christ.

love poem for Jerry Falwell

I believe hell is a real place, where real people spend a real eternity.

—Jerry Falwell

Acknowledging the space between us, greater than the one
between parishioners in the dwindling congregations of
the Baptist churches all across America—
I swear I felt your greasy fist release its grip on history
as He recalled you from the earth like some defective
merchandise. You died on all fours, twisting like a pig
just as you lived by twisting faith like a wet rag
to wring cash into the foul-smelling collection basket
                                                of your mouth.

Hand over your heart, just as
when you praised the Lord for sending AIDS
to punish not just me and those I loved, but
                the entire country for allowing us to live,
                while the applause drowned out our grief.
I too believe in an eternity as yet unseen
by you—sick vaudeville grifter with your fingerprints
writ small across the satellite you stole.
Your mission: witnessing your hate across the planet.

Bible man,
                now that you're dead, I pray
God grant you visions of the world you left
to us, we fancy boys you so despised who,
still alive, are celebrating our survival
                with a sharing of our flesh.

May you witness as the brief fad of the born-again ends,
not with revelations, but with loss of interest.
May you watch with all the fervor of your son
watching the pool boy fuck his wife while you,
your doctrine, politic, and undesired body
                slow resolve like pustule
                rupturing their rot to feed
                                our pretty flowers.

sex dream in which Narcissus lives in your subdivision

The most popular boy in school lives on your street.
Two houses down. You're not friends,
But sometimes in the summer,
when there's no one else around,
you wander in the woods behind your cul-de-sac
together, race your bikes to the convenience store
to buy blue popsicles and cans of coke.
One night, he brings you where the half-completed
skeletons of houses being built for the new subdivision
stand amidst construction vehicles and piles of lumber
in a field of torn up earth.
You sneak across the newly-poured concrete
of a foundation, climb a set of wooden stairs, and there
between two panels of sheet rock, he shows you
how to worship him.
The weather changes and soon school starts up again.
Each year they hold a big assembly in a darkened
auditorium for everybody in your grade to watch
an ancient film on metamorphosis—

FIRST, A FLICKERING PROJECTION OF A BOY STARES
OUT PAST THE CAMERA IN CONFUSION AS NEW MUSCLES
RIPPLE UNDERNEATH HIS SHIRT.

THEN, A GIRL GOES ON A DATE WITH SOMEONE WHO IS
PRESSURING HER TO   *go all the way*
IN THE END SHE IS TRANSFORMED INTO A LAUREL TREE.

By the time the lights come on, you know the word
for what you have become,
what you were transformed into the night
Narcissus took you by the neck and pushed
your head into his lap until you choked.
After school, you go back to the place it happened, but
the house is finished now, and nothing looks the same.
The next day, someone leaves a knife
inside your locker, wrapped up nicely.

Like a gift.

August, almost over

Camp Goshen, 1995 / Orlando, 2018

Midnight and my lover, sad and drunk and stubborn,
won't throw off the covers, so we slowly cook beneath them.

It is humid, but despite the heat we hold each other tightly,
knowing maybe that we're close to letting go.

       August, almost over, always brings me back
to summer camp: the grubby boys crushed
into lean-tos and latrines,
       their damp new bodies giving off a sharp smell
and a dull shine like a distant kerosene lamp.
Yet to be, my young love who now wraps me in his arms.

Unborn, the morning when I saw the head Scout Master
bathing in the creek that ran behind our camp.
Polishing the rough skin of his nude back with
a wet rag while I watched him through a hole
in the mosquito net.
A spy. A bad scout,
       unprepared, my every molecule
       alert with ravishing new ache.
My darling, when he holds me, nothing like that.

But it's sweet still, lying with him. Sweet to be so loved.
I wake up and he's crying in his sleep,
and when I shake him he says,   *I dreamt you left.*

Sweet, the soft curls of his hair, sweat-kissed and black.

Sweet to soothe him, my beloved, through a season soon to pass.

fair

The carnival emerges from the ground outside
your hometown every fall, a cauldron bubbling
over with its bright lights like a buzzing halo
made of noise.

You find yourself surrounded by it:
        Rollercoaster riders screaming overhead
        as music spirals from a distant carousel,
recorded organs playing with familiar cackles
from inside the haunted house, a hall of mirrors
shiny with confusion and delight.

Men call out from the rows of ring toss games
and spray gun races, each competing
for attention, each a brave temptation—
                        then you see him.
Standing in a group of boys,
        the one you wanted most in life.
Not the one you settled for in times of famine.
Not the one whose pity was a thin sheet
on the longest night.
                        No.
Here before you is the boy
        whose sweat-ringed jersey burned a hole
into your stomach, a body like   JOCK Magazine
and name like a novena said while drifting off
to sleep each night.
He looks at you
                and like always you can't breathe.
You want to run, but you can't move
                as he walks up to you and says,

I'm sorry about everything.
Everything that happened.
                Want to walk with me tonight?

It's just you two from then on, together.
Candy apples and pink clouds of sugar
                    melting on your tongues.
The corner store cologne he always wore
is peppering your nose
                    and nobody is staring at you.

No one notices his arm around your shoulder,
or his lips pressed gently to your temple as you
watch the girls who pose for photographs with
pies and doughy piglets
that have won 1st prize.

You stand just like any pair of sweethearts
side by side, in line to ride the Ferris wheel

and as you rise, he wraps you in his jacket,
and you're not afraid, not even as your car
detaches from the rim and floats away.

            The world around you shrinks
            and then collapses like a circus tent.

He pulls you close and points up at the sky,
the endless dark descending on you

                    like a warm quilt,
and whatever it was
            they found face-down and full of pills,
whatever bled-out husk of suffering discovered
in your bathroom, gathered to be dressed
            and laid out peaceful in a box—

            That wasn't you.

            That couldn't have been you.

oh homophobia! up yours!

Thrash me crush me, beat me 'til I fall
I wanna be a victim for you all
                    —X-Ray Specs

There's no term for hatred of my people
that does not contain within it an excuse

for all that scurries from the world's mouth
slick with drool and naked, reaching

with its jagged claws to scratch
the eyes out of the men I love.

If I say,

I do not feel safe in non-queer hospitals,

            or

I remember vividly discussing gay sex with my mother
before I came out; her disgust was tangible,

            or

I was a legal adult before gay sex was
decriminalized in the United States,

If I say,

There are more jokes about prison rape than
depictions of affection between two men in media—

            or

There has only been one openly gay person to win
an Oscar for acting in the history of the Academy—

            or

I have a terminal degree in a creative field.
I was my program's only gay person.
I was also the only person who complained about it,

29

If I say,

Kevin Hart

or

Nancy Reagan

If I say,

*I've dropped out of polite society
because everyone is so breathlessly
homophobic—*

I cannot complete the sentence without
first considering, out loud, the feelings
of my oppressor.

Phobia.

Fear.

I'm afraid
most straight people need
more time to investigate fear,

by which I mean

I wish them the terror
of my youth as educator.

If I am to be held captive
by my own distrust
of what does not love as I love,

then may religious bigots
and officious hypocrites

cower before the idea
of being seen
by me.

A woman scorned,   the saying goes
                         but the man who said it
probably never met a fag
who pays attention to the shit
                  that people say.

       It is a thankless job to slash
       your wrists and splash what
       acid boils from the gash
       into the faces
                   of these beasts
       but it is mine.

I've bound and gagged men twice my size.

       I've made complete strangers
       break down on public transit.

You have no idea
            what I am capable of.

the evidence speaks for itself
Statuette of 2 Gala Priests, 2450 BCE

In life, we served the goddess Ishtar (known
            as Innana to the Sumerians)
who stole the seven powers from the deep
primordial sea Abzu and brought them back
as jewels to shower on our heads. Among
            these seven arts, forbidden sacrament—
a thing you might call prostitution, though
we gave ourselves to Kings and holy men
with love. In life, we built the pleasure house
            of Babylonian Prometheus.
In life, we served our god through ecstasy.
In death, we serve as a reminder of
your birthright: sex, a soft and gilded crown
the patriarchs would hammer into chains.

gay for pay
for "Logan"

nine years
staring at the ceiling
before finally
the golden boy slips
from the earth
and tumbles
into darkness.
nine years wasting
in a body men
   would kill for,
body men would die
   to get inside.
nine years
since they broke him
 in with violent lust.
nine years
since they broke
into his skull
 with kick
 and fist
 and bone shards
 eased themselves
 into the soft meat
 of his brain.
 they say he did
 the skin flicks
 for the money—
   suffered thrust and ran
his tongue across
  calamity for cash
 and yet I find it
strangely unbelievable to make
a trick of it:
    to have men,
    be had by men,
serve their appetites

                while free
of instinct's grabby hands—
            and still
they say it wasn't   sex.
they say for once,
        a handsome cocksucker
left scrambled in a gutter
for something other
than the grave-piss of his
simply drawing breath.
nine years
simply drawing breath.
paying fag debts
        for the paid fag sex.
spoon fed bold sweat by the camera.
spoon fed soft food by his mother.
nine years
nine years
and the studio took down his pictures,
paid down bills for house calls
                    from the doctor,
one last man   to search his body
                    for some sign of life,
        some spark.

who we are
after Ke$ha

It's senior year and everybody has a crew, even the fags like me: the trickster gods of small town southern high school, pleather trenchcoats and velocity. Tonight, cell phones are new technology, and iPods still a dream, so I will almost crash my car three times while trying to switch the music on my Discman from Tori Amos to a different Tori Amos. Tonight my girl Kixie has stuffed herself into something obscenely gold, a too-tight lycra tube top, teenage tits defiant, slicked with glitter, stockings ripped all up the sides, a spider web. Tonight I'm wearing white eyeliner on my lips because I want to look my best for Russ, the hunky goth boy from the trailer park, gray storm clouds for his eyes. His best friend Josh and my friend Charlie are racing shopping carts downhill. Tonight they'll break their ankles; meanwhile Mikey works his magic to five-finger an entire sewing machine. But we steal more hearts than DVDs tonight—and we steal a lot of DVDs tonight. Loud mouths smacking Diet Mt. Dew like snorting NoDoz in the gas station bathroom, like, *Hey, we're going to throw a rave inside this abandoned house we found off Rt. 17, do you want to come?* Like Party City glow sticks, battery-powered boom-box, roadside candy necklaces and so much hairspray. Tonight we live to devastate our haters, leave two flaming tire treads across the face of everything
that wants us dead—

They want us dead.

This place, it swallows all the queer that it can catch. I watched so many of us drowning trying to cross the river that surrounded my hometown I swore I'd only cross it once—to leave. And isn't that just like a witch, to take off like you're being hunted? To know their god for who he is, and still got Jesus on my necklaces— this is who we are. Who we are. Who we are: standing at the intersection of Hot Topic and hot merchandise, rebel yelling against the angry white suburban mob. Tonight we're going in. Tonight we're going hard. Tonight the world is ours. Tonight we're going to light the sky illegal with our firecrackers, kicking glitter in the face of all the varsity perfects. Tonight we let the cool kids burn. Tonight, we're tearing down their posters, tearing up the back roads, tearing up our jeans, and tearing up these speeding tickets. It is senior year, motherfuckers! Everybody has a crew especially young fags like me: too sick for the doctor, too fabulous for hell. Tonight we crank the stereo so loud, to sing along we have to scream. Tonight, tonight, and every night forever when we hear that music play,   we live   we die   we rock   we ride again

while you've been away
for D. Blair and Little Richard Penniman

The Architect took his last breath today.
I watch the world choose from which angle
they will view his life, but I remember you
    evangelizing, so nobody would forget
a small town queen invented rock & roll.

I hate the way death comes for our people—
suddenly, and bearing all the accolades
that might have saved our lives.
How many are so eager to possess
    our newly-sexless bodies.
You left quickly, but it took me months to claim
the loss—in soft and sotto flashes, bottle passed
between us on the floor of a hotel room, lips left
    traces wet like a swift kiss,
the fragments of a conversation. On a bus ride
between Boston and New York you said
    something about god still loving us
that I can't quite recall.   Then you were gone.
I loved your mind, the times when we were just
two faggots talking shit about the boys who
haunted us by night, the seedy bars and last stops
before somebody's motel, and always
    with the lights off.

But if there is a thing like grace, you had it.
Chipped tooth and a knapsack, Black enough
I had to hail your cab when all those 3rd Ave
motherfuckers should've knelt to kiss your feet.

I learned early how to use my anger, but you
showed me how to wear it: armor in a torn up
army jacket, slung guitar in subway station,
    fresh kicks just ripped from the hearth,
and dancing hard enough that nobody could see
    how much it burned.

villanelle for the wound

The last time I saw Josh at school his head was shaved. His skull was stapled shut. He'd liked this boy, and when the boy found out, he spit on him. Then, 8 months later—out of nowhere—he clubbed him with a metal pipe. Our drama teacher, Mr. Franklin, said, *Remember that forever children; that's what hatred looks like.*   But I saw the wound; it didn't look like hatred. It looked like a mouth.

Wide open mouth, blood rusted gate that let the dreadful animals of lust escape.   How dare he speak of it out loud? Didn't he know what waited just outside the walls for boys like us?   Did he forget? The last time I saw Josh at school his head was shaved. His skull was stapled shut. He'd liked a boy, and when the boy found out,

he spit on him. He shouldered him against a wall of lockers. The boy, whose name was **THOMAS RIVERS**, was convicted of two counts felony assault but skipped the murder rap with something that they called, *the gay panic defense.*   In a panic, he left a boy for dead. *Remember that forever children; that's what hatred looks like.*   But I saw the wound; it didn't look like hatred. It looked like a mouth.

with tarnished metal sutures for its teeth, white puckered scalp for lips, a murder-dazzled brain just barely balanced on its tongue. A loud and punch-drunk mouth that babbled languages of dumbstruck fog and held its smile for my eyes—unbearable. A jagged riverbed. The last time I saw Josh at school his head was shaved. His skull was stapled shut. He'd liked this boy, and when the boy found out,

it was from someone Josh trusted, some girl whose razorwired name is lost to us, who probably thought it would be *funny did you hear about it? Josh, the gay kid, thinks you're cute.   He likes you.   He told me.*   Jealous girl. Jeering hive. A blistering of ants. A vicious, swarming red. *Remember that forever children; that's what hatred looks like.*   But I saw the wound; it didn't look like hatred. It looked like a mouth.

The mouth I kissed instead of David's mouth. Instead of Tim or Adam's mouth. The mouth that swallowed risk and flirt and spouted plumes of dreadful silence. We men who love men's bodies know this mouth. Its whispered menace. Its venomed spit. Its fevered breath. The last time I saw Josh at school his head was shaved. His skull was stapled shut.   He'd liked a boy.   The boy found out. and I remembered that forever.   What it looked like.   Hatred.   Like a mouth.

sex dream in which Antinous thinks you'll look great with bangs

You watch him in the mirror, Antinous
the dying and reborn, while he revives
your wet tangle of hair.
                    His golden shears,
an ibis chirping at your temples as he asks
about your family, what you do for work.
He perks up when you mention travel,
speaking fondly of his time in Egypt
                    hunting lions with his lover,
and it opens you a small amount, to listen
to his voice tread gracefully the melody
        of speech belonging to your people.
Glowing creature, once a teenage boy
the waters of the Nile stole from Hadrian,
the emperor by whom he was so loved,
he was made god and crowned with flowers.
Wreathes of the Egyptian Lotus
                    thrown to him at shrines
        from Carthage to Constantinople,
petals the same fuchsia as the silk shirt
                    that he wears to sculpt you
                    delicately with a blade.
It's love-making, the way he crafts you better
        than before and swipes the bright flame
of the dryer's breath across your neck
and shoulders;   love-making,
the way he baptized you beneath the faucet,
blessedly warm fingers of the water mingling
                            with his own.

the evidence speaks for itself

The Tomb of Khnumhotep and Niankhkhnum, 2400 BCE

Although we were in charge of—wait for it—
    the hairdressers and manicurists of
    Menkauhor Kaiu, a pharaoh from
the 5th Egyptian dynasty, and though
we were entombed, unprecedentedly,
together; though we are depicted as
embracing on the walls of our shared tomb
        of the necropolis at Saqqara,
with noses pressed together in a kiss,
    the scholarly consensus reached by most
        contemporary Egyptologists
is that we are, quite obviously, twins.
They aren't sure how the pyramids were built,
      just that no one gay was there to see it.

ПОДВИГ
for Maxim Lapunov

I hope you will forgive me my devotion,
        impotent, a pinprick
                twisted
into useless rage
        on your behalf at cocktail parties
thrown for academics
        drunk on their American пошлость.

How I would bring
            the cities of their courtesy
            to ruin, but inevitably
            someone cuts me off
            to change the subject.

History
        is what a culture tells itself
when rising from the charred page
of a war to burst
        luxuriant with poetry and song again.

Astonishing,
        to watch our countrymen pretend
they cannot hear the music of our people
                even as they dance to it.

A miracle,
        how still we toil in the service
                    of our nations' joys
        to be paid with such silence.

Hero,

Thank you for refusing them their favorite currency.
Thank you, trading safety for the truth

before the jeweled eyes
      of the same world
swarming with batons

      the last day that you stood
      outside a Honey Festival
         to sell balloons to children.

Rows of market stalls stacked high
with sweetness incorruptible as it is stolen.

This, the more renowned fruit of an insect
      needed most to midwife flowers.

Nothing blooms without them.

      Nothing will bear fruit.

First there is no color, then no life at all.

These too vanish all the more each day,

      from field and headline both.

St. Lucia is not known as a volatile place for homosexuals
—*CBS News, "St. Lucia official apologizes for attack on 3 gay Americans"*

On a night like any in the tropics, three white men
are waylaid on vacation and left bleeding
                                        trust into the soil.
Bats and blades make bruise of them and make off
with their jewelry, sparing lives in stifling heat.

            The island government apologizes overnight
            to audience of international news media.

It's inexcusable, this incident,
like any insult paid to foreign wallet.

            Elsewhere, silence tourniquets the wound
            of Marvin Augustin, 18, found face down

with his throat slashed and skin blistered with
three stab wounds for each year of his small life.

Perhaps here is the proof that faggotry is daylight
in reverse. Unnatural, and rising in the West.

Perhaps that's how despite a lack of local *volatility*,
Augustin knew enough to leave behind the name
                        and photograph of whom he was to meet
on Trouya beach:
                        a man who, when confronted
by Augustin's family, swore innocence but fled
                        from the suggestion of police.

How like a bribe, his picture handed over
                        to authorities and disappeared
            into the ravened darkness of their pockets.

to a new crush

Ok so we like each other that's great you like me I like you I am thrilled I'm thrilled by your arm brushing up against my arm our collarbones almost in flagrante while everybody else is in the kitchen arguing about our civil rights or environmental justice or some shit we sit here camped out on the futon couch talking about our favorite sports cars and watching funny videos I like it here on the couch I like it here with you it's easy to be here with you I like that I like you I like how you laugh I like how you smile I like how your eyes scrunch up like a little cartoon fox when you smile I REALLY LIKE YOU it's ok that we don't have anything in common it's ok we have nothing in common it's fine if we don't have anything in common because you make me feel off balance in the way that only happens when you meet somebody really emotionally unavailable and I would love to have you call me once every 7–9 days like when I'm almost over you call then because I see what you're into you want me to come over to your house and fuck you all night long and then curl up next to you all night long and then ghost in the morning and I'm not into kinky shit like that or maybe I am maybe I'm not sure maybe uncertainty turns me on look I've been single long enough to watch entire porn careers bloom and wilt and now I'm too old to be cast in porn and you are still too young to drink and this is really stupid

    BUT I REALLY LIKE YOU   quick run save yourself go find somebody else some guy your own age to beat you off or beat you up or bake you cookies or whatever the fuck it is you want I don't know what you fucking want why is it always my job to figure out what people fucking want Jesus   WAIT COME BACK I LIKE YOU it's not weird it's not weird that we made out a couple of times and never really talked about it it's not weird it's not weird that I gave you a back massage while you were wearing nothing but a tiny towel and then we were rolling around in your bed and when I bit your ear you said we shouldn't sleep together because you didn't want to lead me on it's not weird it's not weird ok it's a little weird I'm not standing on the edge of a precipice looking down at the gnarled bones of those who died twisted in agony just trying to love you no I'm not afraid of death I'm not afraid of a little arson I'm not afraid of getting burned horribly burned dental records burned no it's fine it's FINE I'm in control I'm in control I'm in control I hate control please take all my power away I want to make love to you I want to make sloppy mistakes in the backseat of your car I just don't want to be responsible for the details later.

I just don't want to stop until the sparky part is over.

The warming-my-fingers-by-the-sensuousness-of-your-hormonal-blush-oh-the-crackling-of-a-forest-fire's-romance-oh-the-scurrying-of-adorable-woodland-animals-that-were-once-my-pride   part.

Oh boy.

My handsome little bottle rocket pressed between my lips.
I'm counting down the seconds until you blow.

I can't wait.

love will be your undoing

You're crying outside of a restaurant
when a man you've never seen before
walks up to you.

> *It's over,* he says. *I don't love you anymore.*

You walk inside and sit down at a dirty table.
The strange man follows, slides
into the booth across from you.
For a long time, neither of you says a word.
He's striking. Just your type. Sad in the eyes.
Thick mouth. Busy hands.
There's a cheap pink vase of plastic flowers
on the table, which he plays with while you
> think about how much you'd love it
> if he tackled you and had you rough
> against the sticky tiles of the floor.

After a while you ask,
> *Do you think we could be friends?*
> *I just don't think we should be together,* he says.

A waitress comes and clears the table.
You wonder if he thinks she's prettier than you.
For a little while, you make awkward conversation.
> Then a hostess brings the menus.
> You sit, reading them in silence.
> *Sorry,* he says, getting up to leave.
> *What happened?* You ask.

He puts on his coat and walks out.
After an hour, the hostess leads you to the door.
> You get into your car.

On the drive home, a song is playing on the radio.
The tune is catchy but the words don't make sense.
The singer is so happy to be in love, finally, but
then her sweetheart leaves her, and she is alone.
Even though it's clear that they belong together.

> Surely that can't be right.

You spend the rest of the week locked
in your dorm room, sitting at your desk, erasing poems.
One day, you are walking to a class when you hear
the man's voice from around a corner.

> He's talking to a friend.

>> He's talking about you.

> *I don't even know him*, he says.

Later that night you walk across campus to his room.
You climb into his bed. He holds you while tears crawl
up your cheek into your eyes like horror movie blood.
When you kiss him for the first time, it feels beautiful
and sad. You see each other for a year in secret.

> You come to his room at night.

> You think about him all the time.

It hurts that nobody can know about you.
When you kiss him for the last time, you're both drunk.

> You go to a house party together to sober up.

> You're both standing in the kitchen laughing

> for no reason when he grabs a dishtowel

from the counter and starts wiping jungle juice
on your white shirt. *It's really fine*, you say.

>> *Oh damn, I'm so sorry*, he says.

You stop laughing. *What's your name?*

You turn your back to him. He bumps into you.

The rest of the juice flies off your shirt and back into your glass.
That's the last time that you see him.

> Finally, you feel at peace.

The hot madness in your blood subsides.
You have a lot of fun at the party. You go home, excited.

> Everything is about to get so much easier.

When you go to bed that morning,
you take off your shirt and fold it up.
You slide it back into the packaging.

> It looks so clean.
> Absolutely spotless.
> Not ruined at all.

lupercalia

I dropped out of school to write songs
and take hits of nitrous, stare at pictures
of him on the internet.
I called him at all hours
                swearing that I loved him,
                begging him to say it back.

I never thought he would,
                but then he did.

                I hated him for that.

So when I spilled about the fifth of vodka
that I funneled down my throat

                the night some dumb suburban dad's
                thick johnson pried my teenage ass apart

when I was half blacked out, I kept him
on the phone to listen as he panicked silently,

then I hung up to crawl under my desk
and sift for fragments of an orange pill
                in the carpet.

                All this just to punish him
                for taking it away: my only fix.

I've never been addicted to a thing
                other than pain—
                sharp zip in the septum from
                a poorly chopped prescription.

Love bites on my neck from silhouettes
emerging from the shadows
                of a cruise park.

Some too-good-for-me boy leaving
all my messages on read.

I blamed him when he left
and shred myself against my own edges.

I hauled my Wurlitzer six blocks on a dolly
to sing murder ballads at the Cutting Room.

I set his old t-shirts on fire in the alley.
Ran around the city,
          screaming,
               suffering,
          alive.

The last I heard, he worked the night shift
in a stockroom for eight bucks an hour,

half his check sent to an ex he knocked up
just a few months after he tried dying—

dragging an X-Acto knife against his neck.
The coward couldn't even force the blade
                    in all the way.

sex dream in which Xōchipilli is an early riser
after Xōchipilli Īcuīc

First, you're nothing—
    then you're born to it, through darkness
born, a chaos pouring into measured chaos,
      bursting bloom of bone and ichor.
Such a story lives
        within the body of all men—
but not a man, your love
    who's left your bed to make the coffee.

Peeling back the sleep in layers locust thin,
    you watch them walk into the kitchen,
    fastening a robe of lemon silk
around their godly body, muscled umber,
overgrown with ink, and leaving
       after
      every
        step
     a trail
     of
     yellow
      flowers.
Some mornings you wake to singing
    in the shower and the voice,
though low, is not a man's,
and though it sings of war
    it also sings of dance and rain,
and sometimes David Bowie lyrics
streaming through the house
      like butterflies.
In certain versions of cosmogonía
    as told by the Mexica,
it's Quetzalcoatl
who escapes the underworld
    and carries in his beak
      remains

of what once walked
the earth in ages past,
        a femur
    which when shattered
and then mixed with blood let from his sex,
becomes the first thing
                like a human being.
Born of wound and accident: a man—
and every other thing,
        somehow a bitch.
    Is it religion then,
                a kind of faith,
this queer creation myth
that's sprouted from within archaic stories?
Does it matter what we call ourselves,
if to the king
            we are all faggots?

    Does it matter how we live if we arrive
        at death along the same sad path?
It matters
        to your love,
        the prince of flowers, not a man,
        who's come back to the bedroom,
        pupils wide and black as the abyss,
            tobacco pipe between their lips.
A paltry offering of words for one who
keeps you safe.
Who brews you tea
            from psychedelic mushrooms,
                packs the bowl for you.
    Who pulls you close and takes you,
                not-girl,   *like a woman*,
        one might say
        if that is what one chooses
            to believe.

Andy's dream

At devotion
    they were told
to picture Jesus
        in the desert
walking
    toward them
with a gift.
Alone
        beside
  the son of god
among the stones
    and sand,
my sweet,
 a child, then
    tore out
his heart
    and threw it
at the savior's
    feet.
It landed
    with a wet slap.
Lay there
    dirt-struck.
In exchange
    the Lord
        gave him
    a cross
so heavy
    he could
barely
    stand
beneath
    its weight.
Afterward,
    some kids
        were

laughing
   thanking
 god
for their new
   PlayStation,
the keys to a
   Corvette.
My darling
  sat
among them,
  quiet.
Andy,
  so much
  of the men
who raised us
  rests
   in god.
  So much
  to be
 undone
  in our
   bed,
  and only
   one thing
in between us
to replace
  what
 you
  have
  lost.
It's
  mine,
   but
  I
  will
 break it
  for
   you.

it gets better, by halves

When you pick your youngest up from school,
he's missing his left ear.   *I left it in my desk.*

He seems embarrassed as he pulls his hat over
the blank stretch of skin, staring straight ahead.

                              Can we go to Taco Bell?

A week goes by and then one of his thumbs is gone.
He rolls his sleeve down to cover his fist.

                         I forgot it in my locker.   I'll get it tomorrow.

But instead the next day all his hair is shaved off.
Then one of his feet goes missing.
                    Then an arm up to the elbow.

It isn't until he climbs into the car without eyes
                    that you begin to worry.

You shake him by the shoulders, asking,   *Who did this to you?*

                         I didn't see,   he says, feeling for
                    the sunglasses tucked in his pocket.

When finally there isn't enough left of him to send to school,
you pour the last pieces into a jar and keep it by your bed.

After dinner you lie down, turn off your reading lamp.
You unscrew the lid and he slides out:

two fingers running through your hair.
A nose that sweetly nestles in between your breasts.

It is, of course, much easier to love these sweet parts.
Easier to understand a boy who never cries
                    or asks for much of anything.

rent boy

for and after Isaac Dunbar

Restored against all death, the son of Tantalus.
   Repaired, save where the Lord of Oceans
presses his blue lips, a shoulder
      made of polished ivory.
That such a god is risen here
     to lap the ankles of a boy once torn
apart and set before Olympus as a meal,
a mortal steady for the ravishing of water,
brown eyes widened with delight
     amidst a rain of pearls—the myth.
But more heroic is the trust
     with which he lay beside the shore
as invitation to the very sea
      once poised above his rendered
corpse with knife and fork.
How like us, the young prince of Lydia,
   by all accounts unearthly beauty
     after having died, to bend Poseidon
      to his purpose with a soft touch.
Like us, how he fashioned
to a gorgeous spectacle the ruined pieces
   of his stolen life with opulent resolve,
    just as we are compelled to fascinate
the powerful with all our luscious trouble.
Maybe that's why I expected more
a timid creature walk across the stage tonight.
Instead, a bold-strut faggot Jagger dazzled me
    to laughter ugly and incredulous when
     surfacing within your audience, a hand
to pass the gaudy plastic
     of a pride flag to you in an arc.
You wrapped yourself in nylon rainbow
     with a face full up of bliss, as if
the prism brought its own sunlight,
     and softer than the king's velvet.

Outside of the club, not quite
teen idol jitters, but I still could barely speak to you
beyond a half embarrassed,   *You are so important.*
What I meant:

We are more difficult to kill, when they can see us live.

That's why they paid so much to keep us out of sight
for all these years. Why now, they pay to keep us
writing quiet unrequited melodies.
I'm tired of these sweeties, each
more nervous than a first kiss, bleeding
for the ears of girls their agents pray will fall for them,
will flood the venues,
hang their posters, pay
with cash and worship.
Isaac, glitter-breathing dragon,
how I love the way you wear your missing tears,
and how I dread the pressure on you
to eschew the label, or else complicate it
soft, disguised
for the more lucrative of appetites.
They hide us from ourselves this way.
They boil off our poison.
Smudge us from the ledger, from the legends—
Pelops, meaning dark-of-eye or dark-of-face,
an innocent rent
limb from limb
and then revived
as swain for Neptune, grey man of the waves.

All this erased
but for a word inspired by his father's hell,
and even then, it's misremembered as temptation,
when in truth, it's torture to be   *tantalized,*
deprived of what is plentiful,
and all around you.
Glory.
Recognition.

Lives made whole
      and brought out from the shadows,
flourishing complete
    and fully human.

I have seen the world, except for this.
                Except for you.
See how the story changes
    when we are allowed back in?

The moral less of folly in defying god,
and more the possibility
of our existence beyond object for consumption,
that we all might someday rise
                beyond survival
to a greater height, and driving onward chariot
of the divine,
      to some place beautiful
      and natural
        and ours,
      and only
        ours.

What's been left to fester with iniquity must
be destroyed—a lesson from the Bible. Why
then, leave the boy face down to kiss the dirt
yet live? Small enough to spare, you might
think. Only queers (as with the places they
infested in the days of Sodom), Byzantine
with time to grow, their flesh a
complication of pursuits after
the wish to know
love—left untended, longing leaves
a vacuum in the eyes that beckons
touch and flickers with seduction.
Let a good man look too long, and
leave his jock dissolved to salt.
So, no alternative except to strike
and split while they are young. To rain
your fury, wrath in hand. God knows
what happens if you turn back now.

§

Less than ten years after sneaking up behind a child, beating him
into a coma, and then spending the remainder of the day at an
amusement park, Thomas Rivers is released from prison. He takes
refuge in a love of dogs. He teaches them obedience. In public, he
will speak out against inhumane treatment of dogs.   *Men are dogs,*
we sometimes say, and yet it seems that Tommy will allow a dog
to love him without fear of violence. It makes sense he would play
advocate to animals some argue ought to be put down merely on
principle but it's still difficult to picture him as open hand of any
kind, although he has stayed out of trouble. Lives a humble life.
Has been with the same girl a long time.   Table scraps.
It's funny, feed a beast enough tripe on redemption and he's liable
to forget. Get comfortable. Get sloppy. He might think if he moves
to a small town in Florida, just off the coast, into an off-white
three unit apartment building on the corner of Beech and Sunset,
he'll be safe   from the past.

sex dream in which Freyr is the jarl of the road

Gold, the withered earth, the dry grass gilt with death
             and quick with lizards, gold their scales,
the tumbleweeds, the western desert giving way
             to boundless fields of grain, and these are gold,
their harvest soon to bring forth golden loaves of bread
from sheaves of wheat and rye.
They ripen in the blind light of July, and gold the sun,
its warping haze to chase
             the drivers of these bright monstrosities
to worship at the shrine of Iowa, the 80 seen for miles.
Gold the letters spelling out WORLD'S LARGEST TRUCKSTOP
bunting strung up to commemorate
             the yearly Truckers' Jamboree.

             Gold details on the 1912 Mack Jr. on display
in the museum, the 1913 VIM White and the Rambler,
amber lights above the wheel wells of the mid-century
Sterling with its gold interior, the bronze grill winking
from his copper eyes—a honey
             walking up beside you, letting out a whistle.

Well, ain't she a beaut'? he says,

        a gold incisor shining in the broad grin breaking
        from his thick beard.
Gold, the lone stud in his ear, the queer side.
It excites you, how he keeps his blond hair
sheared into a mullet, sleeveless white t-shirt
torn open to the ribs, a farmer's tan,
             the Kansas lacing sweet his baritone,
the cut-offs, acid-washed and short enough
             to show the pockets.
Gold, the belt-buckle he shoves his thumbs behind,
             the two men etched across its face,
                 embracing.
He wants you to see the custom Harley
        he's got chained up in the trailer of his semi.

Walking through the crowded parking lot, the people
move aside for him like he's their king.
He buys you both a corndog,
                              drags you to his rig
              and throws the roll door open like a blind.

It's gold, the chassis of his hog,
                              and lustrous.
Gold, the moment that you climb astride the bike
behind him, wrap your arms around
              the warm shaft of his body,
press your nose against his neck to catch the scent
of thigh sweat, rawhide, fresh-cut grass.
He twists the grips of the ignition,
                    and the chopper snorts to fuming life.
There's gold at the horizon
              as he cuts on to the freeway like a scythe,
                    and kicking into gear begins
                    the first joyride you'll take tonight.

the evidence speaks for itself

the poems of the Shījīng, c.800 BCE

Confucius thought enough of poetry
contained within our pages to preserve
our words. Dynastic heritage of Zhou,
the longest reigning line of emperors
in China, we adhere to cultural
traditions otherwise forgotten or
destroyed in the fénshū kēngrú and swept
from bonfire to wind as fading cloud.
Though tenderness between two men would be
erased by gwáilóu the world over, long
before the birth of their Messiah, we
survived the censors of successive kings
and Communists to hide for centuries
within the sacred texts of the Chinese.

why do we even really need gayborhoods again?
for Eric, since you asked

Because I can remember being 21, a mine shaft rich with pills
and arrogance, self-hatred so pure and dark it burned for years—
my only natural resource. I left the oven on all day and all night,
so hot everything I touched was set on fire.

Because faggots have a history in flame
   flaming, what they call us
when we are too loudly or too gracefully
ourselves, and history, our history, a thing gone up in smoke.

Because we were a people once, a culture of abandoned sailors,
nelly gentlemen who carved a homeland from the places men in
power didn't want.
       We loved each other there.
       We found each other.

       Made each other strong.
       Made each other sick.

Because suicide is still a door that most of us will try
and if we're lucky, find it locked.

Because the gardens of assimilation spill with colorless flowers.

Because they are polite most days
but pour our blood into the sewer.

Because, dear boy, like many pleasant things,

     our safety is a lie.

     It's temporary.

Every city a museum of violent street corners
and hidden places they unearthed with shovels
of their money, Jesus and organic groceries.
Stalking us behind expensive baby strollers.

Because family cannot be made of internet alone.

You'd know this if you walked with me where all
the buildings once were owned by eyes that saw
what you see: beauty in the street, the bath house
and the gym, the dancehall, wonder twisting
through the aisles of a bookstore.
Here, a world we built
because the world we were born into
was not built for us.

Because I carry the impossible dream of acceptance
inside of me, mirage disintegrating
into hasty and convenient sex and once
I thought, like you, rejecting who I was
would save me.

Because you're born gay,
and if you're lucky,
you grow up.

If you are very lucky, you grow up
to live within our midst,
a hand to slide in yours,
unflinching, and secure as any key to a front door
turns smoothly in the lock.

method act

This is not the house that crystal meth built, but
it is the one it decorated—
      strands of Christmas lights gone dark,
      the tiles torn up from the kitchen floor
            and shattered,
    shelves of books and records
            ordered alphabetically—
It's 2:30AM when I arrive at your apartment, and
you're vacuuming the carpet with intensity
    the likes of which I usually reserve for things
            like sex.

Relatedly, you've got a studded leather fuck sling
set up permanently in your bedroom.
This is where I sit, my legs swinging beneath me
    like a child at a Rockwellian lunch counter
while I watch you,
while you breathe
        deliciously the white mist as it
slithers from the glass you hold the flame against.
It clouds your eyes until you're lost.

I guess a good friend might do something drastic,
might run screaming from the room,
say something sanctimonious and cruel,
        then storm off to a hotel—
but I am too poor to be that kind of good.

I can't afford another place to stay, and anyway
      I've missed you terribly, so I get quiet,
   look down at my shoes.
I mumble, *Babe, you know you can't do that forever, right?*

Forever is a funny word.
A paradox, a pipe dream.
      Banished by its very definition
      to the realm of juvenile fantasy,

like any perfect drug,
                or the idea that it is possible
                to save someone you love, or
Pegasus—the winged mare sprung forth from
    where the horrid Gorgon's head was severed.
It is said,
            though often we forget,
            she was a woman once.
                So beautiful the gods were jealous.
You were beautiful like that.
            A lion crowned in flames.
It scared me, how you roared for what you loved
                        and how that drug
                            ate holes
                            in you.

It doesn't matter in the end whose fault addiction is.
Blame your junkie boyfriend.
Blame the hateful doctors at the Mt. Auburn ER.
                Blame me.
                Blame you.
Blame the vicious diamonds with their bliss,
                a swift dissolving fog.

reading Anne Sexton waiting for a rape kit in the ER

bold text lifted from Sexton's "Wanting to Die"

Urgent care ward, a fluorescent yellow
suffocation, beacon calling the unfortunates
of Boston to their bandages, a crisis hive.
 While **BALANCED THERE,** queens **SOMETIMES MEET,**
 RAGING AT THE straight world, and its
 PUMPED-UP MOON, LEAVING THE assault
 WE MISTOOK FOR A KISS.

Observe, the way I always try to do, my privilege:
 I am white.
 I am male.
 I will be seen by a doctor tonight. I am here,
having been taught my health and safety
are worth waiting all night in this ugly room.
 Still I wish this had not happened.
Not here,
while my country still believes consent begins
 and ends somewhere around nudity.

I wish I did not love men's bodies so much,
so deeply and so thoroughly I failed to notice
when he took the condom off and risk
blossomed inside of me without permission.

Trust a stranger like the desperate do.
In order to survive, pride banishes my guilt
 and still it **WAITS FOR ME, YEAR AFTER YEAR, TO SO**
 DELICATELY UNDO AN OLD WOUND, TO EMPTY
 arrogance **FROM ITS BAD PRISON** and
repeat like prayer what happened so when asked I won't forget
to curse my body for its welcome mat, what it admits to me,
 though **I HAVE NOTHING AGAINST** sex.
 Sluts **HAVE A SPECIAL LANGUAGE.**
 LIKE CARPENTERS
 WE WANT TO KNOW *WHICH TOOLS.*
 WE NEVER ASK *WHY BUILD.*
This is why I'm here—to ask for tools.

Instead, I'm asked to strip for an examination.
Waspy nurses come to sting me with their anti-venom,
syrup-thick shoved underneath my skin with twisted lip.

                    I DID NOT THINK OF MY BODY
                    AT NEEDLE POINT when I was
                    getting ready to go out tonight.
Tell me why, like any of us,
                    I know not to expect sympathy
from the police officer
who rolls her eyes at me and says,

                    Well that's not really rape, now is it?
        Sure, I left THE PAGE OF THE BOOK CARELESSLY OPEN,
                    THE PHONE OFF THE HOOK AND THE LOVE,
                    WHATEVER IT WAS,   AN INFECTION.
But how I wish that blood tests not feel so inevitable.
That a handsome stranger's blurred smirk not feel so much like
    I told you so   from every book of history, the hospital
                    a swollen breast, brims over with the milk of

Why were you in bed with someone that you didn't know [slut]?
Can you even remember what he looked like [slut]?
What did you think would happen [slut]?

                                        [slut]

                                                [slut]

                                [slut]

Sluts   HAVE ALREADY BETRAYED THE BODY. DAZZLED,
        THEY CAN'T FORGET A DRUG SO SWEET
        TO THRUST ALL THAT LIFE into your guts!—THAT, ALL BY ITSELF,
        BECOMES A PASSION. BUT SINCE YOU ASK doctor, MOST tricks
        I CANNOT REMEMBER. I put on MY CLOTHING, UNMARKED
        BY THAT VOYAGE. THEN THE ALMOST UNNAMABLE LUST RETURNS.

Lust—A SAD BONE; BRUISED, if only to feel something.
                    Anything at all.

the evidence speaks for itself

Pre-Columbian Moche Ceramic, c.700 CE

I wonder, can you drink as joyfully
    from me as I drink from this man, this king
    this font of bygone era's loving thirst?
    Can you pour forth, as I once did, the milk
within your core, to wet the tongue, the hands
        and chalices of one who molded you?
Fertility in water and in death,
    the people whom I served believed in this:
    beyond the living realm, our ancestors
    assured the land's fecundity with love,
    and more specifically, with fucking. No
    surprise then that among the artifacts
    conquistadors reviled most was I—
        a testament to sexual rebirth.

sex dream in which Agni revels in the curse of Bhrigu

Wet maze of a warehouse, glimpse of limbs
in partial light and grasping hands you fight
past, bramble-thick through hot-breath air.

Choking hunger sears within, it drives you
deeper, deeper, past a wall of doors, some
closed in moaning shelter, others open,

empty but for condom wrappers scattered
under folding chairs and narrow beds.
A chattering of temple rats, the shuffled feet
of men with pants dropped to their ankles,
circling the cauldron of his mouth: the Bollywood kamagni,
hearthrob on his knees before these mortals
as he once knelt before Shiva the destroyer,
as he kneels for Soma, his betrothed, the sacred moon.

How foolish men can be.
How arrogant, believing themselves king,
a god, their supplicant.

They spit derision on the black smoke of his hair
while spilling ceaseless offerings of ghee
between his greedy teeth.
You lean in for a closer look. It's marvelous to see him,
jatharagni crawling toward you on all fours.
His fingers, blazing, part your zipper.
Quickly now he drags you shivering into his heat,
and works you to a pyrotechnic finish.
Fevered clouds of gorgeous color bursting,
crowd your vision spectral.
As you stagger back, he chuckles.
Slaps your ass as you depart.

You will return here many times,
but never find your prince again.
Eternal blistering, the torch you carry torrid
as Khandava in the distance.

Our Lady of the Piers

for Venus Xtravaganza

Jersey girl, a vision
     mopping cigarettes and panty hose.
Each night in Chelsea starts like love itself,
     and limps home with a broken heel
          and kissed off lipstick.

Hidden in her bra, a wad of singles
     and a losing lotto ticket—Venus.
Planetary namesake
          candy pink at the horizon.
Mission of the girl who works: to trust
a stranger hungers for a meal served hot.
To make rough trade in unmade covers
of a room let by the hour.
Cash up front and paid under the table
          under the bed
     and left for days, her body.
Necklace of black, bruising jewels presented
by his choking hands.
He pulled her hair until
          it came off bleeding.
Dress torn to the waist, a page
          torn from our history,
    our newspapers, my sisters all,
    these girls unsolved and called
        unwanted by the same pigs
        paying for their time.
  The breeders make   their monsters out
of anyone who dares   to cross
  the space between   the simple-minded
       genders   they have sanctified, each
    a legend, and   a prison, and
        a lie.
But all myths come with their retellings.
Here is mine:

This time, she escapes, our little goddess.
Blinds the beast with her acrylics,
         claws her way out of that seedy temple
         in rip-stockinged sprint of terror
and a trail of blood erased by storm,
      and no stone in the middle of New Jersey
with some man's name on it—   No.

This time as her hair grows back in frenzied
snarl hissing from the root,
             she sheds the rough scales
picked up on the docks and dons
             a sequined gown of green
so gorgeous men get rock hard
              just by looking at her.
Hip-tilt on the uptown 6
       to something cushy on the eastside.
         Spoiled rich white girl
light wafting slowly
through her rooms of haute couture and mirrors.
Prom queen of the new Versace campaign
          with a venomous tiara,
and an emerald spray of acid rain for earrings.

Justice served with caviar, arriving as a lover
with a bright bouquet of tigerlillies in his arms
to beg her,
        Darling, let me
            make an honest woman out of you.

manslaughter

In 1995 Jonathan Schmitz agreed to appear on an episode of The Jenny Jones Show dedicated to secret admirers. During filming Jones revealed Schmitz' secret admirer was his friend Scott Amedure, a gay man seven years his senior.

Humiliated, Schmitz shot and killed Amedure three days later.
He was convicted of second-degree murder.

I can't stand the way
my brother's willing to humiliate himself,
clichés of light bondage, champagne, and
chocolate-covered strawberries.
     Familiar also: silly gay boy
     falling for the small-town simpleton.

Carnal fangs sank deep as bullet-wound
into the flesh,
     he bares the bite marks as they bleed
for talk-show circus,
     tramp clown, pants around his ankles.

The audience, a hail of eyes ripped wide
through cause of death:
         a man who hides his face
inside the hands that will, in days,
         turn murderous,
and leave a body smeared across the walls
of an apartment like a cream pie
         to the face.

crisis actor

White gay men are holding on to the idea they're oppressed because they
desperately want to have something in common with people they betray.

—someone I admired

Set aside the gotcha question of the men in Chechnya, flesh
colored by bruise alone. Forget the boy's head belching blood
against a crowbar in a park ten minutes from my home.

I'm certain you'll agree the fight for marriage was at best
misguided, trivial, and overblown, although I don't know
how you manage to believe that and also believe we are
               not marginalized, materially,   since
marriage is to date our one material victory in federal court.

Instead of rolling out the list of chemicals I down each day
and night to drown out any voice like yours, even when
the voice is mine, declaring my entire life a lie
I tell to get a little closer to you, I'll spend time
reflecting on the subject of my desperation, and on yours.

I'll admit, I've never understood the urge
to be so desperately possessive of oppression, as if it were
               a resource and exhaustible.
I can't imagine
being such a formidable intellect and still lifting my politics
from social media, dismissing out of hand the facts about
self-harm and suicide, addiction, rape and homelessness—

You should know this by now, but I'll say it again here:

       I don't think you're wrong, but worse, half-right.

I walk in a skin like armor, even if I walk, like all of us, alone—
Cutting a path through fields of daylight in between our lives
       where once stood an entire generation of men just like us.

Fucking the same holes.
                       Losing the same plot.

For your consideration

Here's a list of my redeeming qualities:

I'm a thoughtful reader. Educated, broadly travelled.
Good at conversation, lots of fascinating stories
from the road. With time I have perfected recipes
for chicken breast, ambrosia, and a fishless Caesar
salad. I am kind to strangers if not to myself. I am
possessed of an exacting intellect and linguistic
precision which I only use to say mind-warpingly
cruel things to people who have hurt me very badly.
I'm a snappy dresser and a practiced lover—generous
and patient in the sack, and that's a guarantee.
I'm loyal and I'm funny and I always take my meds,
almost always as prescribed. I keep the house neat.
I'm religiously unwasteful. I'm consistent, though
I will admit sometimes I am consistently insufferable.
I've been described as ebullient and also as a
narcissist but I'll let you decide. I'm confident in
your decision. I am confident. A confidant. Trust-
worthy. Not a gossip (don't believe the rumors).
I take good care of myself, hygienically if not in a
more holistic sense. I always smell good and I'm
going to keep my hair. Great teeth. Regularly floss.
Warm, dry hands. Capable of giving medical-
strength rub-downs and not broken yet. Bruised,
bullied, and betrayed, sure. Gun-shy. But there's
gold to pan still from my rivers and I'm quick to
mitigate my pessimism with a wise-crack. I'm
surviving. I roll tidy joints. I'll look you in the eye
after a toast. I'll hold my liquor all night long and
kiss you like a classic movie star once everybody's
gone home. All this could be yours. I am a prize
bull. I'm a puppy in a box. I am husband material,
I'm healing. Look how hard I'm choosing not to die
today, and every day. Just look. Just look at me.
I swear I'm not so difficult to love.   I swear it.

the evidence speaks for itself

Genji Monogatari, 1008 CE

The earliest known novel, I am called.
The hero in my pages, Genji, meets
the brother of a woman he pursued
without success. He comes to love the boy,
instead.   The first protagonist in all
                                recorded literary history,
a man,   makes love to men, and hey, guess what?
He doesn't die. In fact, the emperor
himself regrets that he cannot enjoy
            the love of Genji, first lothario
in all of fiction, queer before the word
was   needed   to   explain   a   natural
phenomena.   In truth the only queer
desire is the one for censorship.

барские шалости

Valerio, my king, I wait for you,
your second coming, here in Paradise
        (the Polish bathhouse, not the afterlife).
I wear a robe of strangers' eyes, and steam
is rolling off my back. I am desired here and ready
to take all of you inside of me again, to die, to feel
my bones crumble beneath your weight,
my face scraped through the dank hair of your tits.
    мой русский секрет,   a black forest of nightsticks
stands erect from Moscow to St. Petersburg. Between us.

When we met, I said,   *Be careful, things are changing,*
    and you told me,   *There's nothing to worry about.*

Now there's nothing at all.
        Just pictures that we sent each other
that December, me in my Midwestern office,
wrapped in wool and vintage furs, the window
full of falling snow and you, the giant
        Christmas ornaments from the display you passed
each evening on the way home from your job.
           I asked about the weather
and the time of day, trying to say anything besides *I want you.*
Muscle queen and corporate attaché,
    a distant beast, a ramrod for the barrel of my gun.
        My wicked rut in Roman Bunker,
stag on concrete floor, your hand reached out
    to catch my head as I lay down
        astride you. Violently I wanted
you the moment that I saw you, and I still do
and I always will.
        I will die wanting you,
          and I will never see you again.

My Darling Bobik—

It's with an exquisite kind of pleasure that I write to you. The idea that this piece of paper will be in your hands fills me with joy and brings tears to my eyes. Yesterday my tortures reached the point where my sleep and appetite disappeared, which very rarely happens. I'm suffering not only from an anguish which cannot be expressed in words (my new symphony I think expresses it very well), but also from a hatred of strangers, some vague anxiety, and God knows what else. My joy, please write to me right away, even if it's just a few words.

Hugging you to death.

P. Tchaikovsky

It should have been a better year, 2001.
A first semester freshman, running
to my classes every morning, napping
   through the afternoons before the night shift
        at my first job as a waiter at a restaurant,
Korean-owned and operated,
           serving mostly a Korean clientele.
I'd get home late,
          get high often, was pathetic
   with new music,
and it seemed that there were pretty boys
          on every corner that fall.
Every night
I curled up in my bed around a different name:
        Marcin,
         Matt,
       Danny,
         Spencer,
      Mack,
       Ramesh.
My neighbor   Mark
          liked to invite me over
         for a glass of wine on weekends
while he worked on paintings for his upcoming exhibit
           in the local coffee shop.
He dimmed the lights and stripped down to his boxers,
        dabbing at his portraits while I watched.
He said he usually worked naked
       to avoid staining his clothes but kept
       his underwear on
       so I wouldn't get   *the wrong idea.*

Once, after he finished painting
         and we both finished our wine,
he made me watch a vhs tape of him skateboarding
    and even skateboarding he only wore shorts.
The wet sheen of his abs in sunlit sweat
          was pornographic.

Once, when we were smoking on the fire escape,
        he caught me staring at a smudge of yellow paint
below his navel where
                some shocks of coarse hair just escaped
the waistband,
                and the hunger for him kicked inside
        so hard, for a second
                                I thought
        I might vomit.
                Hey I'm up here, he said,
                and laughed.

Bobik—

The day you left was sad for me. Just like in a novel, it's been pouring rain the whole time, very wretched weather. It's remarkable indeed that you took with you the good weather and my good mood. What would have happened if it had rained the whole time you were here??! Were you an interesting and intelligent boy, one might have killed the time somehow; but having taken into consideration your dreadful denseness and silliness, I am filled with horror at what I would have experienced in the course of those three days.

Lunch today was fresh mushroom soup (excellent) and the wonderful brisket you spurned.

Kisses to you,
P.T.

Take two wounded doors left open,
                              swinging in between
the day we all imagine ourselves dressed for every morning
and the one we struggle not to drag home on our shoes each night,
and call these Pyotr's eyes—Tchaikovsky, клинский отшельник
quill in hand attempting to compose the music of a soft moan
                              stifled in a pillow.
              Star-crossed river, tributary
                  stripe of blue to fly
                  amidst his country's pride.
How guileless
              his correspondence,
              the professions of his love
                          for men.
Such passion in the ink dried
                  on a score, historical,
                              a triumph;
      in a letter between friends,
                          capital offense.

Despite their walls and all their warring tribes,
      humanity unites in worship
              of the things that faggots make
              and hatred of the things that faggots are—
                              but what are we?

      What's a man when like us he is made
      both stronger and more epicene?

      The failure of the male sex to observe,
                  corrected, then made flesh, then prey
                  to vandalizing envy and such shame
                  it is become an act of daring
                              just to live,
                  to speak such love by name.
And here again is shame: a finger wagging at our agonies,
      reminders that we live within this age of liberation
      while they scratch our faces out with law's last coin.

Shame here,
       in the swathing of their porcine spawn
with martyred cloth in calls
           for our return to darkness.
Yet there are some shards of light
embedded in my palm for Pyotr,
       dead a hundred years, when first I heard his music
and detected in the swelling orchestra familiar
                something.
In between us,
       half the globe and whole of century—
and still I loved him instantly
    and knew him to be like me.

              I was 9.

      Write a law to stop that.

Bobik—

You are not an empty box but rather so full that everything inside you is in disarray. It's strange you're worried about having no achievements to your name yet—what can be expected of a boy still sitting at a school desk? Just be patient. Enjoy your youth, but learn to value it. Read as much as possible. I'm inclined to think you will be either a writer and an artist, or a writer and a philosopher. I've always noticed how profound your thoughts can be.

I'd love to go to Kamenka with you, but I'm behind on my opera, and as of now, I think it will just barely be ready in time. If I thought you really wanted to go with me, I might, but it's clear you'd rather go with your nasty friend Rudka. I'm sure his company will be quite enough for you. Please don't take this as me asking you to beg.

I hug you tightly!

Yours,

P. Tchaikovsky

P.S. Sugar, sweetheart, my golubchik—

I worship your little box!

My brothers, if you will, forgive me
　　　this, my mad confusion,
　　　　　my audacious fugue.
I spent so many years in search
　　　　　of a divine light.
Cursed your name and mine.
I burned
　　the first half of my life
　　　in sacrifice to straight men
and their straight god, though I knew then
　　　　　that they hated us,
just as I know we're hated now
　　　for this, our plumage lunatic,
　　　　　our faggot magic;
hated for the music and the gorgeous dance
we pulled down from the heavens,
　　hated for our grace.
　　　　For what we love
　　　　and how we love.

We're hated for the gods we are
　and hated for the gods we kneel before.

I mourn the youth
　　　　I spent in saintly coma.
How I wish I might have welcomed life
　　　　　with open legs.
I was so terrified of our disease,
　　　so furious at all our suffering.
I am still furious and suffer still,
　　　　remembering
　　　the kindness
　　　　I once held up
　　　　　like a torch.

It hurts me, all the things I could have been instead of angry.

This thing happens sometimes with gay boys of a certain age where we're adopted by a straight couple, especially a straight couple like Sehun and Hwa. Sehun was tall and brawny, class clown vibes but hardworking behind the bar at the Korean restaurant and handsome. I mean stupid handsome. I mean dead ringer for Kye Sang. Pretty like that. All the other waitresses were jealous of Hwa because Sehun was her boyfriend, but Hwa didn't take shit from anyone. I'm not sure why it happens, this thing with straight couples and gay boys. I'm just sure that it happens, and quite often when it happens it seems like the girl is curious about your gay-boy mind or what it's like to live your gay-boy life and meanwhile her boyfriend is just having fun being your pal even if secretly he's trying to figure out whether or not he'd like to fuck you. I'm not saying this is an explicit thing or even that the boys in question realize what they're doing. I'm just saying it's been twenty years and I can still remember one night when the three of us were on the closing shift together rolling silverware. Hwa was curious about my name and what it meant and I said it meant *God's gift* but that no one really pays attention anymore to what European names mean. Sehun stole a couple roll-ups from Hwa's pile when she wasn't looking and then winked at me.

I asked Hwa what her name meant and she said it depended on the spelling, that the characters for Hwa's full name meant *pretty flower* but that everyone just called her Hwa and by itself this meant both *flower* and *fire*.

That's a perfect name for you, I said.
She smiled, and Sehun laughed. Then I asked him what his name meant and he said the same thing about spelling and then Hwa said something in Korean and he scowled and stomped off to fill soy sauce pitchers for the tables. Hwa told me Sehun's name meant *a life of service* but that it was possible to spell it so it meant *talking until dizzy* and that when he was in grade school he had been a very chatty boy and teased for this, and I'll admit, a lot of what I just told you about that night is made up or embellished, but a little while later when I was alone and washing dishes in the kitchen and Sehun came up behind me, wrapped his arms around my waist and placed his hands flat on my chest where breasts might be and squeezed and ground his hips against my back while moaning, that happened, and at the time I thought that he was joking but in retrospect I'm not sure what the joke was since there wasn't anybody else around—

Absence
is
a kind
of music;
this I mean
quite literally.
One
of the first
things
you learn
in music theory
is the lack
of sound
required
to make
song.
It's said a man named Franco thought up the idea of measuring
the size and purpose of each emptiness within a composition.
The symbology he made
to solve medieval
vagueries
of meter,
the foundation
for notation
still
in use
today.
It's by his efforts
we are able
to determine
tempo
without prior
context.
He
invented
the discrete
moments
of

nothingness
we call
a *rest.*
It begs the question: Is the reason why
historically so many homosexuals excelled
within the old academies of music best
explained by lives spent waiting
in a measured silence?
Although as
with any
melody
composed
too
restlessly,
unceasing
quiet
too
is
its
own
brand
of
pandemonium.
Cacophonous,
the missing life
of Eduard Eduardovich Zak,
the Prussian Ganymede
from dust beginnings
stolen
into immortality
as muse.
Eduard of a mercenary beauty such
that it unseated reason—
or so we can only guess
as there are no surviving photographs.
Edya, whose attentions would beget
Tchaikovsky's

Romeo & Juliet Fantasy Overture.

What's left of him:
                    a scant three sentences
        of broken Russian
            in the post-script
                    to a cousin's letter from vacation,
                something about how he spent July of 1870
relaxing, swimming in the Volga east of Moscow
                                nearby Nizny Novgorod.
The rest is drawn for us like a warm bath
                in the sonata's second movement as the strings
reread the woodwind's lines
            amidst hormonal haze of brass.
You hear it:
                    story of doomed lovers, story written famous
                            by a faggot half-millennia ago,
                then taken up again two centuries thereafter
        by another faggot
                who spent most of his life used up
                        by ferocious talent,
                maybe finding
            only for a moment
                    mercy
            in caresses
                from a pretty boy,
                    a pretty
                        faggot.

        Bliss, however temporary, has a sound.

        Tchaikovsky wrote it.

Anatoly—

Today, I finished the hardest part of the symphony, and had some coffee with Lido in that restaurant by the sea and spent a long time collecting sea shells. On the way back, a fog suddenly descended and was so thick that it was literally impossible to see two steps ahead of us; we went off course and got lost. The cold was brutal.

It's now eleven o'clock. As usual at eight o'clock we had some tea. At nine o'clock I felt like cruising and went out. Some ruffiani, *you know the kind, guessed what I was looking for and wouldn't leave me alone. The bait they were using to hook their prey (i.e. me) was a pretty little thing, nearly irresistible, but in the end, I didn't let them get the better of me. I don't know whether they were trying to blackmail me or just rip me off, but I wasn't fooled. Still, what a dreamboat that boy was!*

Until tomorrow, Tolya. Big kiss!

P.S. Please don't worry, I ever so solemnly swear,
I'll never let me get the best of me.

Ted was selling drugs
                    between his classes
at a famous college for musicians
                    when we met.
He dropped acid
                    with such a frequency
                    it bordered on sublime.

He was profoundly disliked by the local poetry scene.
He signed up for the open mic each week
under the stage name

                    Fuck Human Rights,

and always read the same unsexy material
about sex he had almost certainly not had—

but still,
                    he looked just like this boy I used to know,
                              and always seemed a little lost.
I wanted to protect him, and that made us friends.

          Sometimes when I was in Boston,
                    he would put me up at his.

He taught me how to hot knife wax
                    when even halfway decent bud
                    was still a chore to get ahold of.
          Once,
                    he got me so high
                    that I passed out
                              on his floor mid-sentence.
          Once,
                    when he was visiting New York
                    we planned to meet up at a tea house
                              in the Village.
          He was late,
                    and brought some girl with him who,
                    like most girls who trail the boys
who choose to spend their time with me, was shy

and seemingly unable to contribute
                          to the conversation,
                          even when encouraged.
For some reason
Ted wanted to talk with me
                about sex,
                          more specifically
                about kink,
                          which he was starting to explore.

He talked about an older woman
                          who invited him to her house
                          for a leather fetish party.
        How he was the youngest person there by far.
        How he'd been the star
                that night, the one
                        that everybody wanted
                                        to tie up
                                        and abuse.
        She was like a leather cougar, he said.
                                        It was really hot.
        But something there,
                        beneath bravado,
looking for an explanation of what he had done,
or what had been done to him,
                                reassurance
                                that he needn't be ashamed.

He asked,   *Have you ever been with someone, y'know, old?*

When I was 19 (Ted's age then),
                                white-blond, baby-powder soft,
        I'd wandered
                through the tall grass of the Fens
                where men like me encountered one another
                                        naked in the muddy reeds.
        I told him, carefully,
                about the nights I'd gotten drunk and taken home

by men with thinning hair
                    and grasping hands.

I wanted him to understand that it was possible
                    to be afraid of what we found
when we went searching for an answer
          to the endless questions of our deepest want.

What's a cruise park?   he asked.
I started to explain,   and then
               his friend (who had been silent until now)
                              let out a little titter.
Just imagine my restraint,
               the way my fist went white beneath the table
                              and I didn't lay her out.
I didn't tell her
               that the only reason she was even there
               was Ted's fear that he might end up gay
               if we spent too much time together.

Instead I changed the subject,
                    and then later
                    paid for both their meals.

My dear brother—

Thank you for news about Zak. Your concern for him is quite touching; you have a kind heart. I want to ask you, since you want to keep Zak from traveling in the winter, would you consider giving him a short vacation in the near future? Could you let him or perhaps just tell him to come to Moscow? I would be so glad if you would. I've missed him and I've been worried about his future. I'm worried he might become bitter, or lose the will to get better. I'll be honest with you, if he seems to be in any way declining morally or mentally, I'll take measures to find employment for him elsewhere. Be that as it may, I simply must see him. For God's sake, please arrange it. If nothing else, he needs to see his mother.

I kiss you.
P. Tchaikovsky

P.S. I agree with you, it's time for you to leave Ukraine.

I hate the past.

Inconstant as it is unchanging,
our regret persists while history
itself is ever shifting, constantly
rewritten at the whims of power.

March 1870.

The last notes of the overture bleed out into the air
over the heads of its first audience.
It's spring in Russia, each day warmer than the last.
Tchaikovsky's muse is wearing the same uniform as
every other boy at the Academy of Moscow.

Csar-approved, the heavy black wool military-style
jackets blur as shadows do, the crowd of students
leaving through the front gate at the end of class.

Biography is like this, great men dressed to hide
amongst the ordinary in the service of their pride.

Everyone I know wears the same sadness
but for different reasons.

If we are to be undone by grief, what does it matter
how it comes to pass?
My logic here suggests the opposite
of what I know is true,
that we are, all of us, our most alive before a mirror.
Why else would I be so moved,
imagining Tchaikovsky standing by his window
watching young men passing in their matching coats
and pointed hats in search of one
whose slipping through his fingers
stirred a masterpiece.
Within the love theme's wild return,
I hear an anguish that I understand.

String instruments,
                    as primitive as they are delicate,
just pieces of once living objects
brought together masterfully—a felled tree polished,
                    struck with beastly hair.

What shivers from within is sorcery,
but what of it to you,
        whose want knows nothing of the government?

Who pins a medal on the son that kills
        another man and burns the letters
                of the one who would allow him pleasure.
You
        for whom we're made to read the fairy tales
about Tchaikovsky writing *Romeo & Juliet* for anyone
besides the boy he loved,
                    who loved him,
                        and then died of it.

Vasily, My Gracious Friend!

I'm extremely grateful to you for your letter, and I'm so glad our opera is going on. Regarding the role of Morozova, couldn't you invite Kadmina? She is a wonderful actress and a most sympathetic singer. I have another big favor to ask of you. I am presently affected by a tragic catastrophe that has befallen a person close to me, and my nerves are awfully upset. I am in no condition to do anything. Therefore I ask you not to hurry me with the piano pieces. You shall surely have them, but I cannot guarantee that this will be in the near future. Just wait for two or three weeks. Farewell, thank you for all your troubles.

Yours, P. Tchaikovsky

Which the wound more vicious—from the blade
or from assurances that you have not been stabbed at all?

Am I to be burned alive inside a theater,
trying to find the most believable way to shout   FIRE?

If I say
          a man choosing to love another practices
          the art of haunting some place he has never been,
if I say
          tenderness between them is itself a ghost,

          does the cliché hollow the bones of it until at last
it's capable of flight, if still attended by such wickedness
to circle over men like me,
                              like Pyotr,
                    like Eduard Zak,
                              his last meal hot black powder
                                        and a bullet?
Faster than the speed of music.
                              Gone out with a bang.

It seems our stories always end this way, but then again
          it seems we never have the chance to write them.

Libraries still line their shelves with falsified biographies,
                    conspiring to hide us from each other,
                              from ourselves,
their pages stuffed with lies
                    to make them all more comfortable
                              with what they did to us.
What they still do.
                    It might be funny if it weren't so deadly,
                    all the desperate surgery performed

to make a straight man from the ruined scraps
                    of what is left after our early deaths.

4th September 1887

Last night, before I went to sleep, I thought long and hard about Eduard. I cried and cried. Looking back, it's amazing how vividly I can remember him. The sound of his voice, the way he moved, but especially well I remember the dreamy look on his face that time in the flower garden. He blamed me, and at times I was to blame. It seems unimaginable that he is gone. That he does not exist at all now. I can't comprehend it. I don't think I've ever loved anyone as much as I loved Eduard. My memories of him are sacred to me. God, it doesn't really matter what I tell myself; faced now with his memory I feel such horrible guilt, but I loved him. I still love him.

Tell me of a thing more hunted than the faggot's heart.

Tell me softness in a boy is not pursued from childhood
by every race and every culture, every living god on earth.

Tell me that our histories erased do not amount to rape.

That there is nothing of their envy in their hate,
                            and nothing of their hate
in footage of a chesty woman in a bathing suit
devouring a discount cheeseburger over Tchaikovsky,

or each time it's played to mock the longing
of a clown so ugly, the idea he could be wanted in return
or welcomed anywhere—
                            inherently hilarious.
A joke that kills itself.

Tell me that I made it up each time:

            Valerio gone missing as his country slowly
            turns its back on genocide against our kind.

Mark's heavy pour and fresh cologne.

        Sehun pleading with me not to quit the restaurant.

Ted pulling out a mattress to sleep on the floor beside me
with his face inches from mine.

            Tchaikovsky, whom it's said perished of cholera
            despite the rumors he was made to kill himself
            in order to preserve the reputation of his school
                after seducing the wrong rich man's son.

Russia,
            famous for its use of poison.
            Death from arsenic identical in symptom
                    to a death from cholera, but faster,

just as Pyotr's death was faster.
Pyotr,   whom they sometimes claim
           wrote most his music for a woman he met twice,
and otherwise is cast as slight and pious, tortured and afraid
of what he was, ignoring diaries and letters
                          all proclaiming just the opposite,
and these surviving only
by the intervention of a younger brother who adored him,
who himself was gay,
                     and knew best what Tchaikovsky wanted.

As for what I want,
           imagined reader of a future age beyond my death—
let there be left no room
                   for a convenient lapse in understanding.
Know in life I treasured nothing so much
           as the body of another man.

That I have found such joy within our sex
           as to be brought to savage laughter
and ecstatic tears hundreds and hundreds of times.

I regret nothing, but this: that someday, I will stop.

That we may never meet
                   to weigh your leg against my shoulder
                   or to place a kiss against your hip
or take the living meat of you in fist
to wring out every drop of shame in one
                             riotous
                             almighty
                                   howl.

the evidence speaks for itself

Shake-Speares Sonnets: Never before Imprinted, 1609 CE

Shall I compare thee to a summer's day?[1]

1 It is important that we recognize
what modern readers of The Bard would call
a summer's day, would not, as such, make sense
to those who lived in Shakespeare's time. In fact,
the Pope himself had only just approved
the New Style Calendar (what then was known
as the Gregorian) some thirty years
or so before, which means it's possible
this famous line was written prior to
a common understanding of discrete
unchanging seasons. What we can confirm
is Shakespeare wrote the poem for a man.

more than sex, I miss the movies
New York City, 2020

     The dreams of lonely boys begin there,
hemmed with glass and splashed
                  with light and distance.
    The screen feels too close in my bedroom
          as I boot up a romantic drama
and I roll up two Israelis
             and I smoke them in the dark.
For a minute, I feel like a man,
thighs heavy in grey sweatpants,
           screen staining my bare chest
             with its waves of color.
It might not seem like much, but
I have come to love my body,
though its golden hour passed
         before I was prepared to capture it.
To love now is to paint from memory.
I wish I could show you what it felt like
to believe that it was out there:
                  A place.
A life where men like me
could find each other just by looking.
I wish I could show you what it felt like
         to believe and then to not.

what is and is not written on the back of the VHS

WE SEE HIM SKATEBOARDING THROUGH THE STREETS BEFORE LYING DOWN ON THE DIRECTOR'S BED the wide thighs of a straight boy spreading *You ready?* TO WATCH A STRAIGHT PORNO VIDEO. from an off-screen VCR *You want to see more?* a woman's moan slides thick *Girls want to suck this.* as cold butter across a skillet HE'S ALL ALONE IN THE ROOM, the pleasure is fake *It's a big dick.* but the scream is real WITH JUST THE CAMERA reflected in his dead eyes *Is it big enough for you?* AND YOU WATCHING HIM. Can you see me, Tony? *I want you here, right now.* HE FONDLES You took the money HIMSELF THROUGH HIS CLOTHES 20 years ago *I want you to have it.* FOR A WHILE you made a choice *I want your ass.* BEFORE STRIPPING DOWN AND OILING UP HIS BIG ITALIAN SAUSAGE. a grease fire *I'd fuck you over and over* this mad beast fever burning just beneath the skin TONY NOT ONLY LIKES TALKING to lead me DIRECTLY TO YOU, *You want to come with me?* HE REALLY LIKES TALKING your slave DIRTY. *I've never put it in somebody's ass.* I have SEVERAL TIMES nothing *You like this dick? I bet you love it.* no plan HE GETS RIGHT UP INTO THE CAMERA no way out *One like this makes you cum.* AND TELLS YOU to live HOW GOOD IT FEELS *I'm so close to coming* I'm so lonely for you STROKING HIS COCK *so close* so lonely AND ALL THE THINGS HE WANTS YOU Please *Do you think you could deep throat it?* TO DO TO IT *I bet you could take all of it. You want it?* Please *I'd fuck you long and hard* destroy me AFTER ABOUT 15 MINUTES *you want to come with me?* OF STROKING AND DIRTY TALK, fill me *I'll let you know when I'm going to come* my arms are empty *I could come fuck you.* my bed is empty *I think I could.* TONY SHOOTS A HUGE LOAD: I am empty ONE STREAM HITS HIM ON THE CHIN. *I got it all over me* I promise *god my face* if you hold me *my chest* HE WIPES HIS CHIN OFF WITH HIS ARM I will catch you AND AFTER TELLING YOU HOW GREAT THAT CUMSHOT FELT, if you're still alive *how'd you like the porno?* meat hustler *you've got your own come for me, don't you?* HE LICKS THE CUM RIGHT OFF HIS ARM! *It was so good.* come find me. *I hope you enjoyed it.*

sex dream in which you witness the parousia of Tu'er Shen
after the Shījīng

Not like Zeus,
          compelled by magnitude of splendor
to make love in a menagerie of bestial disguises, nor
the Christ, appearing as an infant
          or a corpse according to his whim—
although it's said the Shen of queers was born a man
condemned for crime of blasphemy,
          regarding appetite above the law,
        and slipping through the snare of death,
    began appearing in our dreams disguised as prey.
No bigger than a fist and pepper black,
    the Prince of Rabbits dashes in between your legs
and bids you follow down a path
that leads into a forest where He waits for you:
         the Slaughtered Peeping Tom, Dàyé.
The Secret King
      grown large on centuries of prayer, resplendent
tapestry suspended inches from the ground,
white jade His cheek against the jet mess of His hair,
and wrapped in an immense robe of blood silk,
one sleeve torn and fraying
to a spray of loose threads,
         each connecting lovers yet to meet.
A mystery, how still they search the doomed earth,
just as He once searched an officer undressed
for mercy and found only power, just as you
began to rifle through your sleep for meaning
         and found only symbolism,
and the Lord of Leverets finessing music
    from a Southern fiddle at the center of a clearing
         for a gathering of long-eared ghosts.
They scatter, startled as you shiver in the cold.
He lowers his bow, waves you from the shadows, but
you won't move.   *I am naked*, you say.

Come forth, he commands.
   I will not suffer you ashamed, nor without clothes,
but share my long robes with you, just as we share enemies.
Be not afraid, though they are strong and countless,
      they can never win.

He pulls you close and wraps you in His satin heat.

At last you see Him as He was in life:
a love-struck soldier
  nursing ardor, hidden hard
    as stone within a bitten peach,
     its nectar streaming
      amidst crimson ribbons
       from his pretty mouth.
No beauty can survive a blind world, says The Master,
      nor any ugliness.
The moon above escapes the clouds.
The grass around you, silver, crowds
     with little phantoms.
None the more divine than these, He says,
   who chose to love amidst such hatred.

Every god falls dead before such courage.

jacking off to my dead boyfriend

Anyone who says they don't have mainstays—
moments that they reach for with a slick hand—

is lying. I don't know if dead boys lie, but
I'll lie with you, my ashen prince, oh, any time.

A yellowing love letter unfolded is your mouth.
I don't think I'll ever know a softer kiss,

and softer still is this, your ghost beside me as I
harden thinking on your belly, lean and heaving

underneath me, squeezed between my knees.
My sweet, I can't know if you'll hear me,

but still deep, so deeply your rut echoes to my bones
as it explodes. With joy, I moan your lost-boy name.

See how quickly my bold votive blows out
for the beds we broke. I pray this way for you.

I pour myself out like a bottle on your grave.

Since the beginning of recorded history there have been efforts to write us out of it. The same bastards who debate the existence and importance of our past are similarly invested in suppressing our present struggles for adequate medical care, sexual freedom, and dignity. Listed below are texts that helped inform the poems in this book and my politics. May they inspire a more meaningful sense of Pride and encourage you to pursue radical acts of scholarship.

EARLY HISTORY AND MYTHOLOGY

On Tu'er Shen: Yuan Mei, *What the Master Would Not Discuss, 1788. Shījīng. English & Chinese.* tr. Xu Yuanchong. 2012, China Intercontinental Press. See also Michael Szonyi, "The Cult of Hu Tianbao and the Eighteenth-Century Discourse of Homosexuality," in *Late Imperial China*, vol. 19 no. 1, 1998.

On Bhrigu: *Agni Purana*, c. 11th century CE.

On Xōchipilli: Various, *Rig Veda Americanus. Sacred Songs Of The Ancient Mexicans*, ed. by Daniel G. Brinton, 1890. See also Fray Bernardino de Sahagún, *Historia general de las cosas de nueva españa*.

On Freyr: Saxo Grammaticus, *Gesta Danorum, Book VI*, c. 12th century CE. English tr. by Oliver Elton published under the title *The Nine Books of the Danish History of Saxo Grammaticus*, 1905 (Norroena Society).

On Narcissus and Ameinias: Conon, *50 Narrations* [summarized by Photius], c. 36 BCE. An English translation of Photius can be found at topostext.org. A version of the Greek text is online at remacle.org, digitized by Marc Szwajcer. For a scholarly treatment, see Malcolm Brown, *The Narratives of Konon: Text, Translation and Commentary of the Diegeseis*, 2003 (Beitrage Zur Altertumskunde).

On Pelops: Apollodorus, *The Library, with an English Translation by Sir James George Frazer*, 1921 (Harvard University Press).

On Hadrian and Antinous: Fernando Pessoa, *Antinous: a poem*, 1918 (Monteiro & Co). For a scholarly treatment see Craig A. Williams, *Roman Homosexuality*, 2010 (Oxford University Press).

On Lupercalia: *Corpus scriptorum ecclesiasticorum latinorum*, 1866.

CONTEMPORY GAY LIFE & DEATH

Koji Ueno, "Mental Health Differences Between Young Adults with and without Same-Sex Contact: A Simultaneous Examination of Underlying Mechanisms," *Journal Of Health And Social Behavior*, vol. 51, no. 4, 2010.

Mai Sato & Christopher Alexander, "State-Sanctioned Killing Of Sexual Minorities: Looking Beyond The Death Penalty," Eleos Justice, February 2021. (This report was produced in collaboration with Monash U. and the Capital Punishment Justice Project.)

Spencer Cox, "Living On The Edge: Gay Men, Depression and Risk-Taking," Medius Institute for Gay Men's Health, 2006.

Michael Hobbes, "Gay Suicides Are on the Rise. This Epidemiologist Explains Why." *HuffPost*, June 5th, 2019.

Addis, Samia et al. "The Health, Social Care and Housing Needs of Lesbian, Gay, Bisexual and Transgender Older People: A Review of the Literature." *Health & Social Care In The Community*, vol. 17, no. 6, 2009.

Allan Bérubé, "How Gay Stays White & What Kind of White It Stays," in *My Desire for History: Essays in Gay, Community, & Labor History by Allan Bérubé*, ed. by John D'Emilio & Estelle B. Freedman, 2011 (UNC Press).

Amin Ghaziani, "Why Gayborhoods Matter: The Street Empirics of Urban Sexualities," in A. Bitterman and D.B. Hess (eds), *The Life and Afterlife of Gay Neighborhoods*, 2021 (Springer, Cham).

Greggor Mattson, "Bar Districts as Subcultural Amenities," *City, Culture and Society*, volume 6, no. 1, 2015.

Christopher T. Conner, "The Gay Gayze: Expressions of Inequality on Grindr," *The Sociological Quarterly*, vol. 60, no. 3, 2018.

On continuing anti-gay violence in Chechnya, the superb Elena Milashina at Новая Газета (Novaya Gazeta) has been singularly fearless in covering atrocities largely suppressed by mainstream Russian and international media. Her work can be found at novayagazeta.ru under her Russian byline, Елена Милашина.

FILM AND MUSIC

The films of Gregg Araki have been instrumental in developing the sensibility that informs these poems. *The Living End* (1992) and *Nowhere* (1997) are great starting points for exploring Araki's oeuvre.

James Somerton's "The History of Queer Baiting," a three-part YouTube series, provides valuable analysis of gay representation in film. See especially his helpful history of Hays Code restrictions in the section "Part 1 . . . The First 100 Years."

"Gabe Fucks Logan," Corbin Fisher, August 2019.

Isaac Dunbar, *Evil Twin*, 2021(EP). Trust me.

PYOTR ILYICH TCHAIKOVSKY

Abridgements and composites of Tchaikovsky's letters and diaries are used in "барские шалости" originals found in the following:

Marina Kostalevsky, ed, *The Tchaikovsky Papers: Unlocking the Family Archive*, tr. Stephen Pearl, 2018 (Yale University Press). This volume includes greater evidence of Tchaikovsky's homosexuality, material often elided from previous collections and archives.

Modeste Tchaikovsky, *The Life & Letters Of Peter Ilyich Tchaikovsky*, 1906. This collection of letters, compiled by Tchaikovsky's brother Modeste, is more conservatively curated for the sensibilities of straight culture in post-revolutionary Russia.

П. И. Чайковский. Дневники 1873–1891 ed Ippolit Tchaikovsky, 1923 (State Publishing House). Translations my own.

The Tchaikovsky Research Project in Klin, Russia was invaluable in research related to this project and has been working doggedly to make information about the composer's life and works available for free to the public since 2006. Their English-language resources can be found at https://en.tchaikovsky-research.net/.

See also Dan Healey, "Masculine Purity & 'Gentlemen's Mischief': Sexual Exchange & Prostitution between Russian Men, 1861–1941" *Slavic Review*, vol. 60, no. 2, 2001 for further historical context.

ABOUT THE AUTHOR

Internationally recognized for his work in poetry and theater, Sean Patrick Mulroy is an author, activist, and multi-disciplinary artist from the American South. An award-winning writer and literary educator with a diverse academic background in media analysis and cognitive psychology, his one-man show The Pornography Diaries has been featured on festival stages all over the world. *Hated for the Gods* is his first full-length publication in over a decade, and represents years of research into the history of gay rights and politics at home and abroad, from prehistory to the present day.

If you enjoyed *Hated for the Gods*, the author recommends the following books also released by Button Poetry Press:

AUTOPSY BY DONTE COLLINS

As graceful as it is cruel, Donte Collins' *Autopsy* is a delicate and dangerous text on grief and sexuality. In the tradition of poets like Patricia Smith and Rachel Mckibbens, Collins embraces and beautifies the brutality of experience and the physical manifestations of emotion within the body.

NEW AMERICAN BEST FRIEND BY OLIVIA GATWOOD

In *New American Best Friend*, Olivia Gatwood shapes stanzas of lust and loss with the same undulling blade. The pages spill over with her love for other women, by turns sexual and sisterly, personal and categorical; complimented, yet unbothered by the thrill and fear of her experiences in loving men.

BUTCHER BY NATASHA T. MILLER

Natasha T. Miller's *Butcher* is a truly intersectional text exploring not just Blackness, Lesbianism, or Womanhood, but rather the endangered, enduring combination of all three. Like the titular Black Butch, these poems are sensitive and kinetic; they are defiant with truth, daring you to look away.

OTHER BOOKS BY BUTTON POETRY

If you enjoyed this book, please consider checking out some of our others, below. Readers like you allow us to keep broadcasting and publishing. Thank you!

Desireé Dallagiacomo, *SINK*
Dave Harris, *Patricide*
Michael Lee, *The Only Worlds We Know*
Raych Jackson, *Even the Saints Audition*
Brenna Twohy, *Swallowtail*
Porsha Olayiwola, *i shimmer sometimes, too*
Jared Singer, *Forgive Yourself These Tiny Acts of Self-Destruction*
Adam Falkner, *The Willies*
George Abraham, *Birthright*
Omar Holmon, *We Were All Someone Else Yesterday*
Rachel Wiley, *Fat Girl Finishing School*
Bianca Phipps, *crown noble*
Natasha T. Miller, *Butcher*
Kevin Kantor, *Please Come Off-Book*
Ollie Schminkey, *Dead Dad Jokes*
Reagan Myers, *Afterwards*
L.E. Bowman, *What I Learned From the Trees*
Patrick Roche, *A Socially Acceptable Breakdown*
Rachel Wiley, *Revenge Body*
Ebony Stewart, *BloodFresh*
Ebony Stewart, *Home.Girl.Hood.*
Kyle Tran Mhyre, *Not A Lot of Reasons to Sing, but Enough*
Steven Willis, *A Peculiar People*
Topaz Winters, *So, Stranger*
Darius Simpson, *Never Catch Me*
Blythe Baird, *Sweet, Young, & Worried*
Siaara Freeman, *Urbanshee*
Robert Wood Lynn, *How to Maintain Eye Contact*
Junious 'Jay' Ward, *Composition*
Usman Hameedi, *Staying Right Here*

Available at buttonpoetry.com/shop and more!